ANGLICAN FOUNDATIONS SERIES

THE SUPPER:

CRANMER AND COMMUNION

BY NIGEL SCOTLAND

The Latimer Trust

The Supper: Cranmer and Communion © Nigel Scotland 2013
ISBN   978-1-906327-20-0

Cover photo: ©   Renáta Sedmáková - Fotolia.com
Published by the Latimer Trust November 2013
The Latimer Trust (formerly Latimer House, Oxford) is a conservative Evangelical research organisation within the Church of England, whose main aim is to promote the history and theology of Anglicanism as understood by those in the Reformed tradition. Interested readers are welcome to consult its website for further details of its many activities.

The Latimer Trust
c/o Oak Hill College
London N14 4PS UK
Registered Charity: 1084337
Company Number: 4104465
Web: www.latimertrust.org
E-mail: administrator@latimertrust.org

Views expressed in works published by The Latimer Trust are those of the authors and do not necessarily represent the official position of The Latimer Trust

Foreword to the Anglican Foundations Series

The recent celebration of the 350th anniversary of the 1662 *Book of Common Prayer* has helped to stimulate a renewed interest in its teaching and fundamental contribution to Anglican identity. Archbishop Cranmer and others involved in the English Reformation knew well that the content and shape of the services set out in the Prayer Book were vital ways of teaching congregations biblical truth and the principles of the Christian gospel. This basic idea of '*lex orandi, lex credendi*' is extremely important. For good or ill, the content and shape of our meetings as Christians is highly influential in shaping our practice in following the Lord Jesus Christ.

Furthermore, increased interest in the historic formularies of the Church of England has been generated by the current painful divisions within the Anglican Communion which inevitably highlight the matter of Anglican identity. In the end our Anglican Foundations cannot be avoided since our identity as Anglicans is intimately related to the question of Christian identity, and Christian identity cannot avoid questions of Christian understanding and belief. While the 39 Articles often become the focus of discussions about Christian and Anglican belief (and have been addressed in this series through *The Faith We Confess* by Gerald Bray) the fact that the 1662 *Book of Common Prayer* and the Ordinal are also part of the doctrinal foundations of the Church of England is often neglected.

Thus the aim of this series of booklets which focus on the Formularies of the Church of England and the elements of the different services within the Prayer Book is to highlight what those services teach about the Christian faith and to demonstrate how they are also designed to shape the practice of that faith. As well as providing an account of the origins of the Prayer Book services, these booklets are designed to offer practical guidance on how such services may be used in Christian ministry nowadays.

It is not necessary to use the exact 1662 services in order to be true to our Anglican heritage, identity and formularies. However if we grasp the principles of Cranmer which underpinned those services then modern versions of them can fulfil the same task of teaching congregations how to live as Christians which Cranmer intended. If we are ignorant of the principles of Cranmer then our Sunday gatherings will inevitably teach something to Anglican congregations, but it will not be the robust biblical faith which Cranmer promoted.

So our hope is that through this Anglican Foundations series our identity as Anglicans will be clarified and that there will be by God's grace a renewal of the teaching and practice of the Christian faith through the services of the Church of England and elsewhere within the Anglican Communion.

Mark Burkill and Gerald Bray

Series Editors, The Latimer Trust

CONTENTS

Foreword to the Anglican Foundations Series i
Cranmer and the Lord's Supper. 1

1. Cranmer the Protestant Reformer. 2
    1.1. Thomas Cranmer Reforming Archbishop 3
    1.2. Cranmer's changing understanding of Holy
         Communion. 5
    1.3. Cranmer's Prayer Books. 6
    1.4. Cranmer's understanding of Worship 9
    1.5. An affair of the heart. 10
2. A Gospel Meal. 13
3. A meal of common bread and ordinary wine. 16
    3.1. The Issue of Transubstantiation 16
    3.2. Cranmer's Argument against transubstantiation. 17
    3.3. Kneeling and adoration 21
    3.4. Table Fellowship 22
4. A Meal for Fellowship 25
    4.1. Biblical fellowship meals 25
    4.2. Inter-active Fellowship 27
    4.3. Attendance 27
    4.4. New Testament Understanding of Fellowship 28
    4.5. United Fellowship 29
    4.6. Practical caring fellowship 30
    4.7. Covenant fellowship 31
    4.8. Table Fellowship. 33
5. A Meal of Spiritual food. 35
    5.1. Nourishment through faith. 35
    5.2. Consecration by eating and drinking in faith, ... 36
    5.3. Nourishment from the word of God, teaching and
         preaching. 40
    5.4. Sermons provide additional spiritual food. 40
    5.5. 'All other benefits of his passion'. 42

6. A Meal for Remembrance. 44
  6.1. The New Passover. 44
  6.2. Remembrance in the Communion liturgies 45
7. A Meal for Thanksgiving 48
  7.1. A sacrifice of thanksgiving 48
  7.2. Thanksgiving for our redemption and all the blessings of life. 49
  7.3. Thanksgiving often lacking in contemporary Holy Communion services. 50
8. Cranmer's understanding of the Lord's Supper for Today. 52
  8.1. Not an optional Extra. 52
  8.2. Sunday worship 53
  8.3. Greater emphasis on teaching and biblical exposition 54
  8.4. Taking note of Cranmer's understanding of consecration 55
  8.5. More time for eating and drinking the bread and wine. 57
  8.6. A final word... 59

Cranmer and the Lord's Supper.

Most illustrious Prince, I have considered that the Supper of the Lord (which has been violated by many and great superstitions, and turned into gain) should be renovated and restored according to the institutions of our Saviour Christ; and I have considered that all should be performed according to the Divine Word and of the Ancient and Holy Church, the care and instruction of which belong in some part to my office.

(Thomas Cranmer, Dedication to King Edward VI, *A Defence of the True and Catholic Doctrine of the Sacrament.*)

1. **Cranmer the Protestant Reformer.**

In many ways these words of Thomas Cranmer carry an on-going significance because some of the biblical principles and insights he sought to apply to the Communion service he compiled in 1552 have been lost or obscured in subsequent liturgies. For instance, it will be observed that the changes made to Cranmer's 1552 *Prayer Book* Communion by the Restoration in Church in 1662 undermined his understanding of consecration and the nature of Christ's presence in the sacrament. Additionally there can be little doubt that had Cranmer lived longer and had opportunity he would have made other modifications and changes to the practice of the Lord's Supper. Furthermore it is plain that the Communion liturgies of *Common Worship* contain a number of departures from the clear biblical principles that Cranmer had established. It will be argued in what follows that his principles need to be kept firmly in mind as we assess these and any other orders of service which may be offered.

Since the 1662 *Book of Common Prayer* is still authorised by canon for use in the Church of England, its structures, principles and practice will be kept in view in what follows. That said, it will be made clear at any of those points where it significantly differs or departs from Cranmer's biblical principles.

The Lord's Supper or Holy Communion lies at the very heart of Christian worship. Indeed the gospel writers give us very few details of Jesus' teaching about worship save that he instructed his followers to take, thank, break and eat bread and take, thank and drink wine in remembrance of his sacrificial death on the cross. This was to be the New Passover[1] and like its predecessor, the Jewish Passover, it was celebrated in the homes of Christian believers for the best part of three hundred years. However following the Emperor Constantine's conversion to Christ in AD 312 public places of worship

---

[1] For the Lord's Supper as the new Passover see J. Jeremias, *The Eucharistic Words of Jesus* (London, SCM Press, 1966 edn.) pp 41-61. For an opposing outline of the biblical-theological reasons for not seeing the Lord's Supper as the fulfilment of the Passover, see David G. Peterson, *Engaging with God: A Biblical Theology of Worship* (Downers Grove: Intervarsity Press, 1992), pp. 120-26.

were legalised throughout the Roman Empire. It then gradually became the practice of most churches to hold the sacrament in the new official public buildings.

Over time what had been a very simple ceremony in the context of a domestic meal presided over, in most cases, by the home-owner, was transformed into a complicated, elaborate and lengthy theological ritual. In this process the central act of Jesus' Last Supper of corporate eating and drinking slowly and thoughtfully in remembrance of His death and passion was reduced to only a passing moment as each person queued up to receive a morsel of bread towards the end of this ceremony that became known as the Mass.

1.1. *Thomas Cranmer, Reforming Archbishop.*

Thomas Cranmer (1489-1556) became Archbishop of Canterbury in 1532 following the death of William Warham. Cranmer had graduated with a BA in 1511 and MA in 1515 and had pursued an academic career as a Fellow of Jesus College Cambridge. As early as 1521 the University began to encounter the doctrines of Martin Luther and the Continental Reformation, and Cranmer must have been impacted by them. Certainly by the time he became Primate of All England he was a convinced Evangelical who had embraced the doctrines of justification by faith alone, the all sufficient sacrificial death of Christ as the only sacrifice for sin, and the supreme authority of Scripture in all matters of faith and practice. In consequence, he could no longer accept the doctrine of the Medieval Mass which taught that forgiveness was brought about when the priest offered up consecrated bread and wine for the sins of the living and the dead. This led to his determination not only to reform the Mass but to do it in such a way that the liturgy made it abundantly clear to the people that salvation did not come through any ceremonial act but solely through the death and resurrection of Christ.

Cranmer was unable to achieve this goal immediately because although Henry VIII had separated the English Church from the papacy, he remained committed to Medieval Catholic doctrine and practice. However on 28th January 1547 the situation changed dramatically when Henry died and was succeeded by his son, Edward VI (1537-53), who had been brought up by the Seymour family with tutors who were committed to the Reformation teachings of Luther and Calvin. The atmosphere in England was now such that Protestants spoke openly against the sacrament as 'a vile cake to be made God and Man' and the Mass as 'the worshipping of God made of fine flour'.[2] Thus the situation was now safe for Cranmer to bring his biblical convictions to bear on the Roman Catholic Mass and the doctrine of transubstantiation which he regarded as its central error. This teaching had its roots in the writings of some of the early church Fathers who asserted that when the president or priest prayed the Holy Spirit down on the bread and wine they were changed into the body and blood of Christ. Thus in AD 348 Cyril of Jerusalem asserted in his Catechetical Lectures, 'When we have sanctified ourselves with these spiritual hymns, we beseech the loving God to send forth His Holy Spirit upon the gifts lying before us, that He may make the bread the body of Christ, and the wine the blood of Christ. For whatsoever the Holy Spirit touches is sanctified and changed'.[3] This belief in a change in the substance of the bread and wine received formal articulation at the Lateran Council of 1215. Their statement asserted that the whole of the bread and the whole of the wine were changed in their entirety into the whole of the body and blood of Christ. Thus by Cranmer's time it was a widely held conviction that after the priest had said the consecration prayer over the elements, no bread or wine remained on the altar. It was only the body and blood of Christ. By the beginning of the sixteenth century many priests and Christian believers held ruggedly blunt and crude literal views as to how Jesus' physical flesh was contained in the consecrated Eucharistic bread. Cranmer was increasingly angered by what the mass had become as the following passage from his pen makes clear:

> For what else made the people run from their seats to the altar, and from altar to altar, and from sacring (as they call it) to sacring, peeping, tooting, and gazing at that thing which the priest held up in his hands, if they thought not to honour that thing which they saw? What moved the priests to lift up the sacrament so high over their heads: or the people to cry to the priest, 'Hold up! Hold up! And one man to say to another, 'stoop down before'; or to say, 'This day I have seen my

---

[2] M. Davies, *Cranmer's Godly Order* (Chawleigh, Devon, Augustine Publishing Company, 1976) p 88.
[3] Cyril, *Catechetical Lectures*, 23.7.

Maker'; and, 'I cannot be quiet, except I see my Maker once a day?'. What was the cause of all these, and that as well did the priest knock and kneel at every sight of the sacrament, but they worshipped that visible thing which they saw with their eyes, and took it for very God?[4]

During the early and middle years of Henry VIII's reign there were five different versions of the Mass in use in English parish churches including the York, Bangor and Sarum rites.[5] About the year 1543 Convocation decided to substitute a common rite based on the Sarum use. The entire service was in Latin and Cranmer very likely wrote the text during the reactionary years when Henry moved the church back to a more traditionally Catholic position. Although it was never accepted for use, it may well have been this that set Cranmer thinking of the possibility of a common rite in English. He had also been further encouraged in his planning by the Spanish Cardinal Francisco de Quignon (d 1540) who had earlier in 1535 produced a revised version of the Breviary or priest's handbook which became known as the *Breviary of the Holy Cross*. Although it was never officially endorsed by the Roman Catholic Church it began to be widely used and had a considerable impact on Cranmer whose early drafts of a reformed *Prayer Book* followed it in a number of ways.

1.2. *Cranmer's changing understanding of Holy Communion.*

We have to recognise that over the course of time Cranmer changed his understanding of both the nature and practice of Holy Communion. The first clear hint of any change in his thinking came in a letter which he penned in 1538 concerning a certain Adam Damplip. This gentleman was a monk who belonged to a French order in Calais and had rejected the doctrine of transubstantiation. Cranmer commented, 'therein I think he taught the truth'.[6] Following this, Cranmer continued to believe in a real presence of Christ in the sacrament though not specifically in the bread and wine.

---

[4] Cranmer, *A Defence (of The True and Catholic Doctrine of the Sacrament of the Body and Blood of Our Saviour Christ)* in G.E.Duffield (ed.), *The Work of Thomas Cranmer*, (Appleford, The Sutton Courtenay Press, 1964), Ch 8, p 210.

[5] See J. Ridley, *Thomas Cranmer* (Oxford, The Clarendon Press, 1962) p286.

[6] Ridley, *Thomas Cranmer* p 168.

Some scholars have suggested that by the time of his death Cranmer had come to share the views of Swiss Reformer, Ulrich Zwingli, who regarded the bread and wine as no more than bare symbols which conveyed no special grace even when they were rightly received in faith.[7] Such a contention doesn't sit comfortably with Article 28 which clearly states that for those who receive the sacrament 'rightly, worthily and with faith' there is 'a partaking' of the Body of Christ and the Blood of Christ'. However it should not be overlooked that Cranmer lived a further three years after the publication of the articles (1553) and could possibly have changed his views again. The problem in all this is what constitutes evidence for his opinions; in the compilation of the Homilies, Prayer Books, Ordinal and Articles he was assisted by a team of theologians, whose independent influence is not identifiable. The assumption in what follows is that these publications reflect his own beliefs at the time, which may or may not be verifiable. However, significantly at the time of his trial in 1555 he told his judges that he had been converted by Nicholas Ridley to the view that there was only a spiritual presence in the Eucharist.[8]

1.3. Cranmer's Prayer Books.

Cranmer's first move in the direction of reform came in 1548 when following a gathering of bishops and divines which met at Windsor Castle and at Chertsey he published *The Order for Communion*. The printing was completed in March of what was in effect a four page pamphlet intended to be used alongside the traditional Mass. It contained a series of admonitions to those preparing to take the sacrament but the canon or central consecration prayer of the Mass

---

[7] Dix (G. Dix, *The Shape of the Liturgy* (Westminster, Dacre Press, 1943) p 667 and pp 676-677) suggests that Cranmer was a Zwinglian from 1549.
[8] See C. Smyth, *Cranmer and the Reformation under Edward VI* (London, SPCK, 1973) p 25, 'Historians, while generally agreed that Cranmer was a Zwinglian in the last years of Edward VI, are still divided as to whether he did not pass through a Lutheran phase between his conversion from Catholicism and his conversion to Zwinglianism'. See also Smyth, p 34 and 65 where he discusses the influence of John à Lasco on his thinking.

was retained in its Latin form.⁹ The book did however require that Communion be received in both kinds and it included readings and prayers in the vernacular. Then in 1549 Cranmer ventured a step further and produced an entire Communion liturgy in English. Although it was a radical innovation it came to be increasingly regarded as 'a masterly compromise'. Being largely based on the Sarum Mass it still contained a number of unreformed aspects. The most obvious of these was the consecration prayer that still required the priest to place his hands over the bread and over the wine and invoke the Holy Spirit's presence on them that 'they may be unto us the body and blood of thy most dearly beloved son Jesus Christ'. This suggested that it was at that moment of the Spirit's coming upon the elements that they changed in substance.

Despite having claimed the inspiration of the Holy Spirit for the book and made its use a legal requirement from the Feast of Pentecost 1549, Cranmer soon recognised that it contained a number of imperfections. This was particularly brought home to him when the Catholic minded Bishop of Winchester, Stephen Gardiner, declared that it still taught the doctrine of the real presence of Christ in the bread and wine. Cranmer therefore persuaded Martin Bucer (1491-1551) who had been instrumental in forwarding the Reformation in Switzerland and Eastern Germany but was now resident in England, to give his views on the 1549 *Prayer Book*. Bucer, who had become Regius Professor of Divinity at the University of Cambridge, responded in a piece entitled *Censura*. Although Bucer had died before the new *Prayer Book* was published in 1552, Professor A.G. Dickens estimates that Cranmer had acknowledged about two thirds of his objections.¹⁰ His forthright comments contributed to Cranmer producing what was in reality the most Protestant Communion liturgy that the English church has ever used. Among Bucer's criticisms were the vestments to be worn at Communion which were 'the albe plain with vestments or Cope', the instruction that the priest should put the bread into peoples' mouths, 'knocking upon the breast and other permitted [Romish] gestures', the petition

---

⁹ For the text of the 1548 rite, *The Order of Communion*, see C.O. Buchanan, Editor, *Eucharistic Liturgies of Edward VI: A Text For Students* (Nottingham, Grove Books, 1983) pp 3-6.

¹⁰ A.G. Dickens, *The English Reformation*, (Fontana Collins, 1978) p 340.

for the departed in the Prayer for the Church, the permission to reserve communion, and the use of the word 'altar'.

The 1552 *Prayer Book* therefore made a number of significant changes in a Protestant direction. The word 'Mass' was not included in the title of the new service which was now called 'The Order for the Administration of the Lord's Supper or Holy Communion'. In the prayer of consecration there were no longer any manual acts which required the priest to place his hands over the bread and wine. Nor was there any prayer invoking the Holy Spirit to come on the bread and wine that 'they may be unto us the body and blood of Christ'. The words spoken while the bread was received were changed from 'The body of our Lord Jesus Christ, which was given for thee, preserve thy body and soul unto everlasting life' to 'Take and eat this in remembrance that Christ died for thee and feed on Him in Thine heart and be thankful'. Similarly the words spoken during the reception of the wine were changed from 'The Blood of our Lord Jesus Christ, which was shed for Thee preserve thy body and soul unto everlasting life' to 'Drink this in remembrance that Christ's blood was shed for thee, and be thankful'. Thus there was now no suggestion of any real presence or that the bread and wine were the body and blood of Christ. Put another way, there could be no suggestion of any physical or bodily presence of Christ in the elements following the consecration prayer.

Cranmer's 1552 *Prayer Book* remained in use until Edward died and was succeeded by his Roman Catholic half-sister, Mary, in 1553. She returned the nation to thorough-going Roman Catholicism. However, after only a brief period of five years she died and her half-sister Elizabeth, who was to rule England for more than forty years, re-introduced the Edwardian book in 1559. During the Protectorate under Oliver Cromwell the *Prayer Book* was abolished in favour of a *Directory of Public Worship*. However with the restoration of the monarchy under Charles II, Cranmer's 1552 book was re-instated (though with one or two significant changes of which he would not have approved).

It seems clear that in all these changes between 1548 and 1553 Cranmer was simply moving the church on in a process of evolution rather than revolution. He had learned from his own observation of the times that rapid change often causes people to dig their heels in and stand in opposition, but to move things forward gently by stages gives at least some time for adjustment. Cranmer articulated this wise approach in his essay 'On Ceremonies' which follows the Preface to the 1552 *Prayer Book*. 'Some', he wrote, 'think it a great matter of conscience to depart from a piece of the least of their Ceremonies, they be so addicted to their old customs'. Others, on the other hand, 'be so new-fangled, that they would innovate all things, and so despise the old that nothing can like them but that is new'. Thus Cranmer went on to say that 'some ceremonies are therefore put away because they were 'burdensome' and gave rise to 'superstitious blindness' and others 'are retained still' for the reason that 'they set forth God's honour and glory' aiding the people 'to a most perfect and godly living, without error or superstition'.[11] Cranmer therefore brought in his revisions over time and in a manner that the majority were able to embrace. The Roman Catholic scholar, Michael Davies, has suggested that he had planned his reforms in four stages:

> *Stage one* was to have certain portions of the unchanged traditional Mass in the vernacular. *Stage two* was to introduce new material into the old Mass, none of which would be specifically heretical. *Stage three* was to replace the old Mass with an English Communion service, which once more, was not specifically heretical. *Stage four* was to replace this service with a specifically Protestant one.[12]

Davies went on to state that 'the psychology of this process was very sound'.[13]

1.4. *Cranmer's understanding of Worship*

Cranmer, together with other Christian believers, knew well that commitment to Christ is a two-way relationship in which worshippers draw near to Him and He draws near to them. Worshippers for their part 'Love the Lord our God with all our heart, mind, soul and strength' and in response receive His strength and provision for their

---

[11] Of Ceremonies Why Some be Abolished and some Retained, *Second Prayer Book of Edward VI*.
[12] M. Davies, *Cranmer's Godly Order* (Chawleigh, Devon, Augustine Publishing Company, 1976) p 91.
[13] Davies, *Cranmer's Godly Order*, p 91.

needs. In our times of worship this plays out in two ways. We come humbly acknowledging our sins before Him, aware that 'we have erred and strayed from his ways like lost sheep'. But we also come into His presence mindful of who He is: 'Almighty God our Heavenly and most merciful Father'. He is the ever generous Lord who supplies those things that are necessary 'as well for the body as the soul'. So we come first and foremost to honour Him as we lift up his name and 'set forth His most worthy praise'. But more than that we also come into His presence in gratitude, seeking to listen to His voice and for direction as the Bible is read and explained to us.

In response to our coming to worship the Lord in this way we also receive 'great benefits at his hands'. These include all those things which are 'necessary for both the body and soul'; the blessings of forgiveness, peace of mind and heart, strength to live a new day, protection from danger, guidance 'in all our doings' and the strength to do 'always that which is righteous in his sight'. In Cranmer's Communion liturgy the same pattern is plain to see. The congregation gather 'to laud and magnify his glorious name' as they 'lift up their hearts' and voices in worship and give Him thanks 'at all times and in all places'.

The Lord 'pardons and delivers us from all our sins' and 'confirms and strengthens us in all goodness'. The congregation comes 'weary and heavy laden' but He gives them rest and refreshment. We receive not just 'the remission of our sins' but 'other benefits of his passion'.

1.5. *An affair of the heart.*

In all of this, Cranmer, together with most early Edwardian Evangelicals, recognised that Christian Commitment, and indeed Christian worship, is essentially an *affair of the heart*. This of course derives directly from the teaching of Jesus who so clearly emphasised that true worship is 'to love God with *all your hearts* together with our minds, soul and strength'. The 'heart' in Scripture, as the great New England theologian, Jonathan Edwards, so clearly demonstrated in his book *The Religious Affections*, is that part of the person which has to do with the feelings, emotions and sensory perceptions. It is here in the human spirit that God's Spirit is pleased to live.[14] The apostle Paul in his letter to the Ephesians prayed 'that Christ may dwell in your *hearts* by faith'.[15] Jesus himself distinguished the heart from the mind urging that you 'shall love the Lord our God with all your *heart* and with all your mind...'.[16] The same emphasis is found in Romans 10 where Paul wrote: 'If you confess with your mouth and believe in your *heart* that God raised him from the dead, you will be saved. For it is with your *heart* that you believe and are justified'.[17]

The implications of all this for worship finds particular emphasis in Cranmer's Communion service. It is there in the very first collect which begins by reminding the worshippers that before Almighty God '*all hearts* are open' and goes on to ask Him 'to cleanse the thoughts of *our hearts*'. In the rehearsing of the Ten Commandments, after each one is read, the people's response is to ask the Lord 'to incline our *hearts* to keep this law'. In the Prayer for the Church Militant the congregation ask that 'with *meek heart* and due reverence they may hear and receive thy holy word'. In the prayer for the Monarch the congregation is invited to pray that the Lord will 'so rule the *heart* of thy chosen servant' that he or she 'may above all things seek Thy honour and glory'. In the General Confession, the people 'earnestly repent and are *heartily* sorry'. Then in the verses and responses following the Comfortable Words the congregation are invited to 'lift up *your hearts*'. It the reception of the bread each communicant is invited to feed on the presence of Christ 'in *thy heart* by faith'. The service ends with a blessing that the peace of God will 'keep *your hearts* and minds in the knowledge and love of God'. Following this there are six collects which are for use after the offertory when there is no Communion, the third one praying that the words which we have heard may 'be grafted inwardly in our *hearts*'.

In this understanding of worship Cranmer was not only emphasising what Jesus had taught but what has been and ought still

---

[14] Romans 8:16
[15] Ephesians 3:17.
[16] Matthew 22:37, Luke 10:37.
[17] Romans 10:9-10. Other references to the heart that bear on worship include Psalm 119:11, Matthew 13:19, Ephesians 5:19.

to be the central aspect and core of Christian spirituality. It was Augustine, Bishop of Hippo in North Africa, who once said, 'O God our *hearts* are restless until they find their rest in Thee'. It was John Wesley who declared that a Methodist is 'one in whose *heart* the love of God has been shed abroad'. John Henry Newman may have begun his career as an evangelical clergyman in the Church of England and although he eventually joined the Roman Catholic Church and became a cardinal, he never entirely parted from his early roots. When he became a Cardinal in the Roman Catholic Church he chose as his motto 'heart speaks to heart', recognising that truth and more importantly that the very presence of God resides in the feelings.

The chapters which follow in this short book aim to make Cranmer's understanding, teaching and practice of the Eucharist clear. It is also the intention to demonstrate the relevance of Cranmer's convictions by suggesting ways in which his principles and practice could be applied by today's church. The study is based on Cranmer's 1552 *Prayer Book* which with a few minor but significant changes became the 1662 *Prayer Book* that is still legally authorised for worship in the Church of England to-day. If we are truly loyal and committed Anglicans this book should be central to our understanding of the Eucharist, and together with Cranmer's other writings should shape our thinking.

2. A Gospel Meal.

Baptism and the Lord's Supper are often referred to as gospel sacraments for the reason that they both illustrate in 'outward and visible sign' the saving death of Christ. In baptism the going down into the water, the burial under the water and the coming up out of the water, serve as a visual picture of the death, burial and resurrection of Jesus. In the case of the Lord's Supper, the elements of broken bread and outpoured wine represent Jesus' body sacrificially given for us and his cleansing blood poured out for our forgiveness. One thing that is immediately apparent when we read *Cranmer's Order for the Lord's Supper or Holy Communion* is his emphasis on this fact that it is a meal which enshrines the good news of the gospel in the way that no other meal does. His liturgy puts great emphasis on the depth of our human sinfulness, the need for forgiveness and the all sufficient death of Christ to make atonement for our wrongdoing. There is also a strong focus on faith and the importance of the Scripture. The service is in fact structured in a way that it conveys the Gospel message. It begins with a full acknowledgement that we have fallen short of God's ways and the recognition that we need God's mercy. This is then followed by the General Confession in which 'we do earnestly repent' and beseech God to 'have mercy upon us'. After this is done, we come in faith and trust to receive the forgiveness which comes through the all sufficient sacrifice of Christ. Cranmer in fact revised the structure of the 1549 liturgy so that in his 1552 book (and the later 1662 version) there is not even a hint of offering, or self-offering, or even a sacrifice of praise until AFTER receiving the bread and wine.

The grievous nature of human sin is underlined in a number of places in Cranmer's order of service beginning with the rehearsing of the Commandments immediately following the Collect for Cleansing. After each petition the people respond with the words 'Lord have mercy upon us and incline our hearts to keep this law'. In the first exhortation after the Prayer for the Church Militant those who plan to partake of Communion are urged 'to search and examine their consciences in order that they may come clean to such a heavenly feast'. In a later paragraph 'hinderers and slanderers of God's word' along with adulterers are to 'repent you of your sins or else come not to that holy Table'. In the Invitation which precedes the

General Confession only those who 'earnestly repent you of your sins... and intend to lead a new life' are invited to draw near and receive the sacrament. In the Confession itself we are left in no doubt as to the serious consequences of our sin and the need for forgiveness as 'we acknowledge and bewail our manifold sins and wickedness which we from time to time most grievously have committed'. Such wrong-doing provokes 'most justly the wrath and indignation of God's divine Majesty'. This grievous or serious nature of human sinfulness doesn't stand out quite so strongly in the prayers of penitence in *Common Worship* Order for the Celebration of Holy Communion. As Cranmer saw clearly, it is only as the seriousness of our condition is recognised that we are indeed 'heartily sorry for these our misdoings' and 'earnestly repent' and call out to the Lord 'to have mercy on us for thy son our Lord Jesus Christ's sake'.

In order that no-one should persist in believing that forgiveness might come through the priest offering up consecrated bread and wine on the altar, Cranmer produced a form of consecration which makes it absolutely explicit and beyond all doubt that Jesus' death is 'all sufficient'. His prayer heaps phrase upon phrase to impress this supreme and vital truth on the hearts and minds of the communicants. Jesus' death was 'once offered' and therefore cannot be repeated in any Mass or Eucharistic ritual. It was a 'full, perfect, and sufficient sacrifice, oblation, and satisfaction for the sins of the whole world'. Since Jesus' death was, and indeed is, all these things, there is absolutely nothing we can offer, add or contribute to our salvation. In other words, as Luther and the Reformers taught, we are justified by *faith alone* apart from any works on our part, a teaching which is in line with Galatians 2:16 that 'we are justified by faith in Christ and not by observing the law', along with other passages in the New Testament.[1]

Cranmer's supreme stress on the atonement thus enables him to underline the need for faith in Christ alone for salvation. The rubric immediately following the Creed requires there to be a sermon or a reading of one of the Homilies.[2] In the Homily entitled 'A Short Declaration of the True, Lively and Christian Faith' Cranmer

---

[1] Romans 4:6, Ephesians 2:9.
[2] Homily of Salvation in *Miscellaneous Writings of Thomas Cranmer* (Parker Society, 1841).

contrasts 'dead faith' which is 'the faith of devils' and 'a faith without repentance' with 'quick and lively faith' which is 'inward and stirreth the heart'.[3] It is this 'quick and lively faith' with repentance which Cranmer urges that we exercise as we eat and drink the wine at the Lord's Supper.

---

[3] *Homily of Salvation*, Part 1, p 135.

3. A meal of common bread and ordinary wine.

The meal which Jesus shared with his disciples in the upper room consisted of ordinary bread and ordinary wine. However a teaching soon began to develop that these elements changed in substance – until finally the Fourth Lateran Council in 1215 spoke of the bread and wine *transubstantiated* into the body and blood of Christ. The key sentence was 'His body and blood are truly contained in the sacrament of the altar under the forms of bread and wine, the bread and wine having been *transubstantiated,* by God's power, into his body and blood'.[1] This theology was later re-iterated by the Council of Trent in the sixteenth century in opposition the views of Martin Luther and other Protestant Reformers. However Cranmer was so convinced that the Eucharist was to be understood as a meal that he changed the title of the service from 'The Mass' to 'The Lord's Supper'. He stood in strong and total opposition to any notion of change in the substance of the consecrated bread and wine. Indeed he laboured the point in both his *Prayer Book* liturgy and in his major theological work entitled *A Defence of the True and Catholic Doctrine of the Sacrament*. The central aspect of the medieval Mass was the doctrine of transubstantiation. But as far as Cranmer is concerned it was ordinary bread and wine at the start of the Communion service and it was ordinary bread and wine when the service came to a close. Indeed if there any bread was left over at the end of the service the minister was welcome to take it home and use it on his meal table.

3.1. *The Issue of Transubstantiation*

The view that after the consecration no bread or wine remained on the altar led to a number of other unbiblical doctrines and practices, the most significant being that the consecrated bread and wine which were now the body and blood of Christ were to be offered up at the altar by the parish priest for the sins of the living and the dead. The actual words of the Sarum Mass, the text which Cranmer used as his

---

[1] See H. Bettenson, *Documents of the Christian Church* (Oxford, University Press, 1967) p 148.

starting point, were as follows: 'We offer this sacrifice for the sins of the living and the dead'. Cranmer asserted that the mass in which the priests made such a propitiatory sacrifice for the quick and the dead was 'the greatest blasphemy and injury that can be against Christ'.[2] Thus what had been instituted by Jesus as the new Passover meal in remembrance of his once for all sacrificial death had with passing of the ages become a sacrificial ritual in which the priest offered up transubstantiated bread and wine, not as a memorial remembrance, but as a sacrifice for sin. In short, the ritualistic ceremonial offering had taken the place of the supreme event it was intended to symbolise and bring to remembrance. In opposition to this change Cranmer is abundantly clear that this was an erroneous unbiblical view and constantly asserted 'that bread and wine remain after the words of consecration' and that the Lord's Supper is what it says in its title, a meal pure and simple.

3.2. Cranmer's Argument against transubstantiation.

Cranmer therefore devoted the whole of the second book of his celebrated *Defence of the True and Catholic Doctrine of the Sacrament* to this matter. It is titled *The Second Book Against the Error of Transubstantiation*. At the very outset, it should be said that Cranmer was clear that when Jesus said, 'This is my body', nothing was more obvious than that his body and the bread he referred to were two entirely different and separate things. Cranmer begins by noting that it was *after* Jesus had given the bread and said 'take and eat' that he then spoke the words 'this is my body'.[3] Likewise it was '*before* the words of consecration' that Jesus took the cup of wine, and gave it to his disciples' and then that he uttered the words, 'Drink you all of this'.[4] Cranmer further reinforces the point by referring to the fact that when the supper was ended Jesus told the apostles that he would not drink 'this *fruit of the vine*, until that day that I shall drink it new with you in my Father's kingdom'. These words, Cranmer urges, make it clear that it was '*very wine* that the apostles drank at that godly

---

[2] *Defence*, Bk 5, Ch 1, p 215.
[3] *Defence*, Bk 2, Ch 2, p 82.
[4] *Defence*, Bk 2, Ch 2, p 83.

supper'.⁵ Cranmer added to this argument with a reference to Paul's Letter to the Corinthians where the Apostle speaks of the *bread* which we break being 'a communion of Christ's body'. This is clearly 'consecrated bread' because the apostle speaks of it as 'a communion of Christ's body' and yet he still speaks of it as *'bread'*. Added to this, he immediately says that the communicants are 'partakers of one *bread* and one cup'.⁶

Cranmer pursues his view that the bread and wine do not change in substance after the consecration prayer with an argument from natural decay. 'The wine, though it be consecrated, yet it will turn to vinegar, and the bread will mould, which then will be nothing else but sour wine and moulded bread, which could not wax sour nor mouldy, if there were no bread or wine there at all'.⁷

It is part of Cranmer's theological method, having used Scripture and common reason to make a point, to go on to cite the writings of the Early Fathers of the Church in support of his argument. Among several who endorsed his views, Cranmer quotes from Irenaeus and Chrysostom. The former stated that 'the bread wherein we give thanks unto God, although it be of the earth, yet when the name of God is called upon it, it is not common bread, but the bread of thanksgiving, having two things in it, one earthly, and the other heavenly'. Cranmer's point is that Irenaeus was of the view that the 'earthly' still remained even after the consecration had been made.⁸ Chrysostom's words hardly need further comment. He wrote, 'The bread, before it be sanctified, is called bread; but when it is sanctified by the means of the priest, it is delivered from the name of bread, and exalted to the name of the Lord's body, although *the nature of bread doth still remain'*.⁹

Cranmer is particularly strong in his denunciation of his fellow English churchmen who in the matter of transubstantiation 'speak more grossly herein than the Pope himself', many of them 'affirming that the natural body of Christ is naturally in the bread and

---

⁵ *Defence,* Bk 2, Ch 2, p 84.
⁶ *Defence,* Bk 2, Ch 2, p 85. See 1 Corinthians 10: 16-17.
⁷ *Defence,* Bk 2, Ch 2, p85.
⁸ *Defence,* Bk2, Ch 5, p 89.
⁹ *Defence,* Bk 2, Ch 5, p 98

wine'. Indeed Cranmer was far from being charitable when discussing the doctrine of transubstantiation as taught by the Church of Rome which he described as 'although in name most holy, yet indeed it is the most stinking dunghill of all wickedness that is under heaven, and the very synagogue of the Devil, which whosoever followeth cannot but stumble, and fall into a pit of errors'.[10]

Cranmer advanced another argument against transubstantiation. He suggested that if Christ's body that was eaten at the Last Supper was made of bread, then Christ's body that was crucified must also have been made of bread. Then by the same logic he maintained that if the body of Christ in the sacrament *was* made of bread and wine, and the body of Christ in the Virgin's womb was *not* made of bread and wine then the sacramental body of Christ is not the same as the Christ who was conceived in the Virgin's womb.[11]

Cranmer also tackled those 'Papists' who 'say that Christ is corporally present in as many places as there be hosts consecrated'.[12] His argument was that Jesus' body and humanity are in heaven and will remain there 'until he come at the last judgement'. Such a conviction he stressed 'hath been ever the catholic faith of Christian people'.[13] The logic was plain to grasp: that if Christ's physical body remains in heaven until the end of the age then it cannot be present in any material sense on a church altar. Cranmer explained this contention with an illustration from the sun. Just as the sun is ever corporally in the heaven and nowhere else, yet its influence and operation can be felt everywhere on earth; so our Saviour Christ is bodily and corporally in heaven sitting at the right hand of the Father while at the same time he is spiritually present on earth.[14] Cranmer rounded off his Second Book by stating that, yes, the bread is changed but 'not in shape, nor in substance'. Indeed the natural substance remains, but another property is added so that it is both 'a corporal food for the body, and a spiritual food for the soul'.[15] He later repeated the argument in Book 3 of his *Defence* asserting that 'his

---

[10] *Defence*, Bk 2, Ch 7, p 102.
[11] *Defence*, Bk 2, ch 8, pp 103-104.
[12] *Defence*, Bk 3, Ch2, p 126.
[13] *Defence*, Bk 3, ch 3, p 127.
[14] *Defence*, Bk 3 ch 2, p126.
[15] *Defence*, Bk 2, ch 11, p 108.

bodily presence is ascended into heaven with his whole flesh and blood, and is not here on earth' and that 'the substance of bread and wine do remain still, and be received in the sacrament; and that although they remain, yet they have changed their names, so that the bread is called Christ's body, and the wine his blood; and that the cause why their names be changed is this, that we should lift up our hearts and minds from the things which we see unto the things which we believe, and be above in heaven'.[16]

Following his usual theological practice Cranmer adds weight to this view with a number of quotations from the writings of the early Fathers. He cites Augustine who wrote, 'We must believe and confess that the Son of God, as concerning his divinity, is invisible, without a body...but as concerning his humanity, we ought to believe and confess that he is visible, hath a body and is contained in a certain place, and hath truly all the members of a man'.[17] Thus, in the words of Colin Buchanan, 'What Cranmer will not stand is any objective location of the presence of Christ in the elements independently of reception. Thus there can be no worshipping of consecrated wafers, no reservation, no processions or other activity which would tend towards such worship'.[18] Cranmer concludes the matter at the very end of Book 4 of *A Defence*:

> But all that love and believe Christ himself, let them not think that Christ is corporally in the bread, but let them lift up their hearts unto heaven, and worship him sitting there at the right hand of his Father. Let them worship him in themselves, whose living temples they be, in whom he dwelleth and liveth spiritually: but in no wise let them worship him as corporally in the bread; for he is not in it, neither spiritually, as he is in man; nor corporally, as he is in heaven; but only sacramentally, as a thing may be said to be in the figure, whereby it is signified.[19]

---

[16] *Defence*, Bk 3, Ch 13, pp 167-168.
[17] *Defence*, Bk 3, ch 5, p 131.
[18] C. Buchanan, *What did Cranmer Think He was Doing?* (Bramcote, Grove Books, 1976) p 6.
[19] *Defence*, Bk 4, Ch 11.

3.3. Kneeling and adoration

John Knox (1505-72) who was one of Edward VI's chaplains and assisted in the final stages of the revision of the Second *Prayer Book*, objected most strongly, as had bishop John Hooper (c1495-1555) before him, to the instruction that the people were to kneel to receive communion. In response Cranmer inserted 'The Declaration on Kneeling' which became known as the Black Rubric, because it was printed in black (unlike the other red 'rubrics' because it was a late addition in the printing process). It included the words,

> Lest yet the same kneeling might be thought or taken otherwise, we do declare that it is not meant thereby, that any adoration is done, or ought to be done, either unto the Sacramental bread or wine there bodily received, or unto any *real and essential* presence there being of Christ's natural flesh and blood. For as concerning the Sacramental bread and wine, they remain still in their very natural substances, and therefore may not be adored, for that were Idolatry to be abhorred of all faithful Christians. And as concerning the natural body and blood of our Saviour Christ, they are in heaven and not here. For it is against the truth of Christ's true natural body, to be in more places than one, at the same time.[20]

When Cranmer was called before the Council to defend the rubric, he found little difficulty in doing so. 'The argument from Scripture', he wrote on October 7, 'was absurd: no doubt Christ and his disciples did not kneel at the Last Supper, but neither did they sit: if we will follow the plain words of Scripture, we shall rather receive it lying down on the ground, as the custom was of the world at that time was almost everywhere, and as the Tartars and Turks use yet at this day'.[21]

Elizabeth I had the Declaration removed from her 1559 *Prayer Book* but it was reinstated in the Book of 1662 with the words '*real and essential presence*' altered to the weakened '*corporal presence*' which did not exclude some form of real presence in the sacrament. The

---

[20] E.C.S.Gibson, *The First and Second Prayer Books of Edward VI* (London, J.M. Dent and Sons Ltd, 1932) p 393.
[21] See Lord E. Percy, *John Knox* (London, Hodder and Stoughton, undated) p 151.

purpose of Cranmer's rubric was to guard against the popular medieval ideas of the mass and altogether to deny Christ's physical presence in the sacrament. So far as Cranmer was concerned the Eucharist is a meal in which the communicants eat ordinary bread and drink ordinary wine.

3.4. Table Fellowship

In order to impress on people that Holy Communion was a meal using ordinary food and drink, Cranmer had doubtless had it in his mind that all altars should be removed from parish churches and replaced by ordinary tables of a domestic kind, tables being the setting for a meal and altars for a sacrificial offering. This at least became the policy in some parts of England, as evidenced by the following events showing that the English Reformers were all in strong agreement with Cranmer on this matter. On 27th March, 1550 after Nicholas Ridley had been appointed Bishop of London, John Hooper wrote to Bullinger, 'He will, I hope, destroy the altars of Baal, as he did heretofore in his church when he was Bishop of Rochester'. Hooper was able to further comment that 'many altars have been destroyed in this city (London) since I arrived here'.[22] In 1551 Edward's Regency Council led by Edward Seymour issued a letter requiring this step to be taken, although their order noted that 'altars in the more part of the churches of this realm, already upon good and godly considerations [be] taken down'. It is not altogether clear but the London diocese may perhaps have lagged behind others in the matter. At any rate bishop Nicholas Ridley was charged 'to give substantial order throughout all your diocese, that with all diligence all the altars in every church...within your said diocese, be taken down, and in the stead of them a table be set up in some convenient part of the chancel, within every such church or chapel, to serve for the ministration of the blessed communion'.[23] The Council's letter gave reasons 'why the Lord's Board should rather be after the form of a Table than of an Altar':

First, the form of a table shall more move the simple from

---

[22] F. Clark, *Eucharistic Sacrifice and the Reformation* (Oxford, 1967) p 188.
[23] *Proclamations* in G.E.Duffield (ed.), *The Work of Thomas Cranmer*, p 234-235.

superstitious opinions of the Popish mass unto the right use of the Lord's Supper. For the use of an altar is to make sacrifice upon it: the use of a table is to serve for men to eat upon. If we come to feed upon him spiritually to eat his body, and spiritually to drink his blood which is the true use of the Lord's Supper; then no man can deny but the form of a table is more meet for the Lord's board than the form of an altar.[24]

When the following year Cranmer published his second *Prayer Book* it was clear for all to see that he had endorsed the Council's requirement because in all the rubrics the word *altar* had been replaced by the word *table*. At the start of Communion the priest, 'instead of standing humbly afore the middes of the altar' (1549) was now required to stand 'at the north side of the *table* (1552 and 1662) with the further instruction that the table having at the time of communion a fair white linen cloth upon it, shall stand in the body of the Church, or in the chancel where Morning and Evening Prayer be appointed to be said'.

The point of this instruction was to make clear that no sacred or holy space is necessary in order to receive the sacrament of communion. The requirement of the priest to stand at the north side of the table meant that he would be standing at the long side of the table arranged lengthways down the aisle or sanctuary with the people gathered round. This is also clear from a number of early woodcuts showing the congregation sitting round the table on which there is a substantial loaf of bread and a large chalice. Cranmer did in fact later allow sitting at Communion in his 1553 *Reformatio Legum Ecclesiasticarum*.[25]

The minister leading the Communion service was no longer to be vested in the robes which had been used in the Medieval Mass but was now required to wear the same robes as for Morning and Evening Prayer. This is clear from the rubric at the beginning of the 1552 Order for Morning Prayer which clearly stated that 'the minister at the time of the Communion and at all other times in his ministration, shall use neither albe, vestment, nor cope: but being archbishop or bishop, he shall wear a rochet; and being a priest or

---

[24] *Proclamations*, Council to Ridley.
[25] Buchanan, *What did Cranmer Think He was Doing?* p 29.

deacon, he shall wear a surplice only'.[26] In order to take away any misunderstanding about the nature of the bread and wine Cranmer laid it down in a concluding rubric at the end of the service that 'the bread be such as is usually eaten at the Table with other meats, but the best and purest wheat bread, that conveniently may be gotten'. Lest there should be any superstitious belief that the consecrated wine had changed in substance Cranmer added that 'if any of the bread or wine remain, the Curate shall have it for his own use'! With this instruction in mind, it is a strange but not infrequent sight to witness clergy consuming all the remainder of the consecrated bread and wine and wiping the chalice clean at the end of the service.[27] In fact in the 1552 rubrics there was no requirement to consecrate additional bread or wine if there was found to be insufficient quantity to serve the assembled congregation. In this probably deliberate omission Cranmer was clearly indicating that it was not any action on the part of the priest or minister that brought about consecration. It should be noted that a rubric was added by the Restoration revisers in 1662 requiring additional consecration prayers and manual acts if any more bread or wine was needed.

---

[26] See preface, An Order for Morning Prayer in E.C.S Gibson, *The First and Second Prayer Books of Edward VI* p 347.

[27] Of course 1662 revised Cranmer's rubric to 'if any of the bread or wine remain *unconsecrated*' so this practice does make sense although it is still misguided! The same is also true of the instruction in *Common Worship*, 'Any consecrated bread and wine which is not required for the purposes of communion is consumed at the end of the distribution or after the service'.

4. A Meal for Fellowship

4.1. Biblical fellowship meals

Cranmer was doubtless aware of the close New Testament connection between the breaking of bread or Lord's Supper and fellowship. The two are clearly linked in the book of Acts chapter 2 where Luke records that the early church gave themselves to the fellowship and the breaking of bread.[1] The early Christians came from an inherited Jewish culture in which fellowship meals were a familiar part. Often the shared eating and drinking were seen as a means of cementing and agreement or covenant. In Genesis 6 Isaac and the Philistine King Abimelech got into a dispute regarding the use of wells. When they finally reached an agreement over the matter they sealed the oath they had taken by sharing a covenant meal.[2] Another obvious example was the occasion in Exodus 24 when God's covenant with the people of Israel was sealed. There we are told that Moses and Aaron met with God and 'they ate and drank'.[3] The eating was a very important part of sealing the covenant. As will be observed in what follows Cranmer recognised that the Lord's Supper is a means by which believers seal their covenant relationship and commitment with Christ. In short, it is a covenant meal which is not hugely dissimilar from that of Exodus 24. Indeed the language Jesus used in instituting the Lord's Supper in Matthew 28:28, 'this blood of the New Covenant', is the very language Moses used in Exodus 24:8, 'see the blood of the covenant that the Lord has made with you in accordance with all these words'.

 It is important to keep in mind that sharing meals and table fellowship was a very important part of Jesus' life. Luke records at least ten meals which Jesus shared with other people. These occasions were not simply for sustenance and socialising, they were meals with a theological or spiritual importance. Such was the case at the Last Supper when Jesus instituted the Lord's

---

[1] Acts 2: 42.
[2] Genesis 26:28-31.
[3] Exodus 24:11.

Supper. As has already been noted, the Lord's Supper was intended to be a supper in the full sense of the word. The practice of sharing the bread and wine in the context of a meal appears to have been widespread throughout the first century. As F.F. Bruce observed: 'In apostolic times it is fairly clear that the Eucharist formed part of the fellowship meal'.[4] In some parts of the Roman Empire the practice continued well into the second century and beyond. Ignatius in his Letter to the Smyrneans wrote: 'It is not lawful without a bishop either to baptise or make an agapé'.[5] The *Didachè* or *Teaching of the Twelve Apostles* knows of no separation between the Eucharist and the Agapé. Section 9 'Concerning the Eucharist' gives thanks 'both for food and drink to men for enjoyment' and that 'you have given spiritual food and drink and life eternal'. It is apparent from contemporary sources that in many places at least until the end of the second century the Lord's Supper was part of a fuller meal called an Agapé or Love Feast.[6] Tertullian of Carthage (c160-c220) wrote of the sacrament of the Eucharist 'which the Lord commanded to be taken at meal times and by all'.[7] The fifth century church historian, Salminius Sozomen, recorded that in a number of cities and villages in Egypt people met on Sabbath evenings 'to partake of the mysteries' after they have dined.[8] Evidently there were occasions when these meetings sometimes got out of hand as appeared to have been the case on some occasions at Corinth.[9] This fact may be the reason for their gradual separation from the Eucharist.

---

[4] F.F. Bruce, *The Spreading Flame* (Carlisle, The Paternoster Press, 1992) p 198.
[5] Ignatius, *Letter to the Smyrneans*, 8.
[6] 2 Peter 2:13; Jude 12. Commenting on Agapé as it appears in Jude 12 P.H. Davids, *The Letters of 2 Peter and Jude* (Nottingham, Apollos, 2006) pp68-69 writes: 'While some writers view these meals as something separate from the Lord's Supper or Eucharist, we are not convinced that the evidence supports that position. Instead, it appears to us that at least until A.D. 250, when the concepts of priest, sacrifice, and altar begin to appear with respect to the Eucharist, the Lord's Supper was a re-enactment of the Last Supper or the fellowship meals of Jesus and his disciples. That is, it was a pot luck meal with bread broken at the beginning and a cup of wine shared at the end'.
[7] Tertullian, *The Crown* 3:3-4.
[8] Sozomen, *Ecclesiastical History*, Bk 8:19.
[9] 1 Corinthians 11:17-34.

4.2. Interactive Fellowship

Considering the emphasis that Cranmer placed on the Lord's Supper as the New Passover it is hard not to believe that had he lived longer and because his theology really was a work in progress that he would have gone on to advocate celebrating communion in the home. He must have known only too well that the Passover was shared by Jewish believers in the context of the home with family members and close friends who gathered and 'reclined' round the domestic table. He would also have been aware that the Passover was a relaxed occasion with the children taking an active part in the proceedings. Indeed the *Mishna* states that the Passover is a joyful, celebratory interactive fellowship meal. The central aspect was of eating and drinking while joyfully remembering the deliverance from slavery in Egypt. This was accomplished by having a number of points at which different foods were shared and bread was broken and eaten and several cups of wine drunk in a relaxed and informal atmosphere.

4.3. Attendance

Significantly the Lukan account of the Lord's Supper mentions more than one cup which suggests a Passover context in which several cups of wine were drunk. Cranmer was also aware that the Apostle Paul clearly saw these same links between the Lord's Supper and the Passover. In his letter to the Corinthians (1 Corinthians 5:7-8) he wrote, 'For Christ our Passover has been sacrificed. Therefore let us keep the Festival, not with old yeast, the yeast of malice and wickedness, but with the bread without yeast, the bread of sincerity and truth'. He was saying in effect that just as the Jews banished the old leaven from their houses before the Passover Festival took place, so Christians are called to live out the New Passover by banishing old leaven style behaviour from their homes. All this is not to say that the parallels between the Passover and the Lord's Supper match in every detail. Indeed, in an interesting passage, Cranmer issued a reminder that the Lord had 'ordained not a yearly memory (as the Paschal lamb was eaten but once a year,) but a daily remembrance he ordained thereof in bread and wine'.[10] In spite of these words it seems unlikely that Cranmer would have countenanced a daily celebration of Communion in each parish church probably for the reason that he wanted people to recognise the seriousness of the sacrament and to come with hearts and minds properly prepared. Perhaps in penning these words he had in the back of his mind the early Christians in the book of Acts who daily shared in the breaking of bread in their homes.[11] In fact the rubric at the end of both the 1552 and the later 1662 *Prayer Book* services state 'that every Parishioner shall communicate at least three times in the year, of which Easter shall be one'. This suggests that Cranmer did not anticipate that Communion would be the main regular Sunday worship service. Indeed, in many places right up to the early Victorian years most English parishes held only three or four communion services a year.[12]

4.4. New Testament Understanding of Fellowship

The New Testament scholar, Oscar Cullman, regarded fellowship and the breaking of bread as two foundational aspects of all worship in the early Christian community.[13] The word fellowship (Greek *koinonia*) has the basic meaning of participation or sharing. The primary focus of New Testament fellowship is the relationship between Christ and his people and then arising out of that there is fellowship among Christ's people, the church. Both aspects are seen at the beginning of John's first letter where he writes 'that which we have seen and heard (namely the life and teaching of Jesus) we proclaim also to you, so that you may have fellowship with us; and our fellowship is with the Father and with his son Jesus Christ'.[14]

---

[10] *Defence*, Bk 3, Ch 12, p 166
[11] Against this view (*The Defence* was published in 1550) Cranmer responded to Bucer's critique of his 1549 liturgy by inserting a rubric into the 1552 order of service exhorting the negligent to attend and adding what seems to be a very minimalist requirement that the minimum attendance should be three times a year.
[12] See for example, N.A.D. Scotland, *Good and Proper Men; Lord Palmerston and the Bench of Bishops* (Cambridge, James Clarke & Co, 2000) p 151.
[13] O. Cullman, *Early Christian Worship*, p 12.
[14] 1 John 1: 3-4.

Cranmer was aware that the Lord's Supper was intended to facilitate both this upward focus of Fellowship with the Father and Son and the horizontal aspect of fellowship between the Christians who gather to receive the sacrament. Thus he viewed the Lord's Supper as *Holy* Communion, which is the sub-title of his service. A meal table is a place of fellowship and encounter. Sharing food with another individual is a way of getting to know them in a personal way and establishing a bond of friendship. Above all else Cranmer regarded the Lord's Supper as an intimate encounter in which first and foremost the worshippers have a deep personal meeting with Christ himself. As the closing words of the Prayer of Humble Access put it we come in order 'that we may evermore dwell in him, and he in us'.

4.5. United Fellowship

In the rubrics at the beginning of both the 1549 and 1552 *Prayer Book* Cranmer laid it down that any who

> have done any wrong to his neighbours by word or deed shall be advertised by the Curate having knowledge thereof in any wise not to presume to come to the Lord's Table, until he have openly declared himself to have truly repented and amended his former naughty life that the congregation may thereby be satisfied which afore were offended and that he have recompensed the parties whom he hath done wrong unto, or at the least declare himself to be in full purpose so to do, as soon as he conveniently can.

Cranmer's rubric clearly resonates with Paul's injunction to the Corinthian church not to contemplate sharing in the bread and wine 'when there are divisions among them'. To do so, Paul wrote in 1 Corinthians 11: 20-22 and 27-32, 'is to despise the church of God' and is 'to eat the bread and drink the cup of the Lord in an unworthy manner' and more even than that, it is 'a failure to recognise the body', (Christian community) which will result in 'judgement' and 'sickness'. Just as the Old Testament fellowship meal could serve as a means of effecting peace and unity among the guests (Psalm 23) so the Communion table provides the opportunity to re-establish a bond of peace with our neighbours and fellow worshippers. Cranmer deliberately returns to this passage in 1 Corinthians 11 at the beginning of the exhortation which precedes the Invitation and the General Confession. He urges all that 'mind to come to the Holy Communion... to consider what Paul writeth to the Corinthians'. He urges them 'diligently to try and examine themselves, before they presume to eat of that bread, and drink of that cup'. He goes on to speak of the great danger if people receive unworthily. By so doing 'we kindle God's wrath against us, we provoke him to plague us with divers diseases, and sundry kinds of death'. His exhortations serve to warn all who are blasphemers, adulterers or be in malice, envy or any other crime 'to bewail their sins, and come not to thy holy table; lest after the taking of that holy sacrament, the devil enter into you, as he entered Judas, and fill you full of all iniquities, and bring you to destruction, both body and soul'.

Although Cranmer removed the kiss of peace from the Sarum Mass he included an invitation to the table in the Exhortation that follows, to those 'that do truly and earnestly repent you of your sins and are in love and charity with your neighbours'. The theme continues in the second prayer after the reception where the communicants pray to 'continue in that holy fellowship and do all such good works, as thou hast prepared for us to walk in'.[15] The same emphasis is found also in the prayer for the Church Militant which comes at an earlier part of the service where petition is made that all that do confess thy holy name 'may live in unity and godly love'.

4.6. Practical caring fellowship

Fellowship in the New Testament was something which needed to be worked out in practical ways between believers. Acts 2:42-47 records what may have been a not altogether successful experiment in communal living in which the believers pooled their material resources and collections were taken to support the poor. Regardless of whether or not the Jerusalem church's sharing is seen by recent scholars in a positive light or not, it demonstrates the practical outworking and expression of the New Testament implications and understanding of fellowship. Cranmer clearly understood the need for this to be expressed in the Lord's Supper.

---

[15] Ephesians 2:10.

Concern that all members of the local body of Christ are loved and provided for was made explicit by Cranmer in the requirement of a Collection for the poor. The curate is required 'to earnestly exhort the congregation to remember the poor'. Such a concern seems also to resonate with the instruction of the Jerusalem church leaders to Paul and Barnabas 'that we should continue to remember the poor'.[16]

This whole aspect of practical concern for the fellowship is one that rarely features in most Anglican Communion services where the focus is most often on individual communion and personal devotion. And yet the importance of a loving and united fellowship was indeed a marked aspect of New Testament social life and worship. Somehow there needs to be an opportunity within the Communion service to facilitate interaction between worshippers in such a manner as to strengthen their bonds of love and friendship. This element was obviously much easier to achieve in the first three Christian centuries when the Lord's Supper was shared by small groups in domestic homes. Nevertheless there are ways in which this could be achieved in a larger context. For example worshippers could be invited to get into small groups of three or four and discuss something they have just learned from the sermon or they could briefly introduce themselves to each other and share some Christian encouragement from the past week as happened in early Methodist gatherings.

4.7. *Covenant fellowship*

The Greek understanding of the word *koinonia* meant more than just interaction, it also denoted commitment. Indeed *koinonia* is sometimes used in Greek literature of people who have entered into contractual agreement or a business relationship. For this reason New Testament Christians would have found it hard to understand the ways in which contemporary Christian people frequently change from one church to another. This deeper form of commitment fellowship is made clear in all four New Testament accounts of the Lord's Supper which record Jesus' words that the cup of wine is 'the

---

[16] Galatians 2:9-10

New *Covenant* in my blood'.[17] When Moses established the Old Covenant between the Lord and the people of Israel at Sinai, he read out all the Lord's words and laws and the people responded with one voice, "Everything the Lord has said we will do". Moses then sealed the covenant agreement by sprinkling the people with the blood of young bulls.[18] Thus the old covenant which was based on words and laws (Exodus 24:3) was sealed in blood. In a similar way the Lord's new covenant was sealed with the blood of Christ symbolised by the Communion cup of red wine. In the third exhortation Cranmer emphasises and calls Christian people to recognise that the Lord's Supper ('these holy mysteries') are 'pledges of his love... to our great and endless comfort' and that they for their part need to continually be submitting themselves 'wholly to his holy will and pleasure, and studying to serve him in true holiness and righteousness all our days'.

This is clearly a crucial aspect and intention of the Lord's Supper that often fails to receive the attention it should be given. It is not often that communicants are reminded that in their eating and drinking of the sacramental bread and wine that they are pledging their love and commitment to Christ and reminding themselves once more of 'the exceeding great love of our Master'. This covenantal commitment to the Lord finds expression in a number of places in both the 1552 and 1662 liturgies. It comes at the end of the Prayer of Humble Access as those who draw near to the table pray that they 'may evermore dwell in him, and he in us'. It is there also in the second post-communion prayer which reminds those who have 'duly received' the bread and wine of 'thy favour and goodness towards us'.

In summarising this point it may be stated that fundamental to Cranmer's understanding was his conviction that the Eucharist is a *fellowship* meal, a fact which he made clear by his use of the title *The Supper of the Lord* in the 1552 *Prayer Book*. This was not a ceremony in which bread and wine were turned into the Body and Blood of Christ and then offered up to God as a sacrifice for the sins of the living and the dead as was the case in the medieval Mass liturgies which were in use in parish churches before 1549. Cranmer was well aware that it

---

[17] Matthew 26:28, Mark 10:24, Luke 22:20, 1 Corinthians 11:25
[18] Exodus 24:1-8

was the biblical context of Jewish fellowship meals out of which the Eucharist had emerged. He knew perfectly well that Jesus had promised to break bread with his disciples in the kingdom and that the early Christians in the book of Acts 'broke bread' in their homes. It was clear to Cranmer that the Medieval church had changed the Communion from a fellowship meal to a ritual but that the congregation should be 'eating' (1 Corinthians 11:20, 33) a 'supper' at a 'table' (1 Corinthians 11: 17-34). He fully appreciated that the Lord's Supper was the New Testament counterpart to the Passover Meal and that Jesus had instituted it during the meal in the upstairs room of a house. Indeed the Proper Preface for Easter Day speaks of Jesus Christ 'the very glorious Paschall lambe which was offered for us'.[19] This was a meal in which the participants ate nothing but ordinary bread and drank nothing but ordinary wine, a focus which resonated with the practice of both the New Testament and the pre-Constantine churches. In the rubrics at the end of the Communion Cranmer underlined the fact that the bread used 'shall be such as is usual to be eaten at the Table with other meats' and furthermore if any is left over of the bread or the wine the Curate may have it to his own use'.

4.8. Table Fellowship.

It was because Cranmer wanted to press home the fact that the Communion and not a sacrifice but a fellowship meal that he made great play of the fact that it took place around a table of 'a decent and honest sort' and not before an altar. Just as no-one would sit at a table for a leisurely meal with those they were at odds with so Cranmer was clear that such a situation must not occur at the Communion table. Thus the curate is to warn those 'who are living in malice or hatred' not 'to be partakers of Lorde's [sic] *table*'. All of this is clearly in accordance with Jesus' injunction that if any of his followers going to worship were suddenly struck by the fact that that a fellow believer had something against them, they were to 'first go and be reconciled' and then come to worship. Once the Minister has ensured that this has been done he can proceed with the service.

---

[19] Proper Preface, *Second Prayer Book of Edward VI*. This Preface was not included in the 1662 *Prayer Book*.

The whole idea of the communicants eating one loaf and drinking from a common cup is intended to be a visual reminder of the oneness of the gathered body of Christ. Those, according to the apostle Paul, who come to the Lord's table at odds with their Christian brothers and sisters are in fact both despising the Christian body and damaging their health.[20] The exhortation following the prayer for the Church Militant ends with a warning to those who 'depart from the Lord's table' that 'they depart from their brethren'. Then immediately before the General Confession the priest invites those 'that do earnestly repent of their sins and are in love and charity with their neighbours to draw near with faith and take this holy sacrament to their comfort'.

---

[20] 1 Corinthians 11:29

5. A Meal of Spiritual food.

Having made it absolutely clear that there is no change in substance in the bread and wine Cranmer then made it plain that as well as eating and drinking ordinary material bread and wine there is also 'a spiritual feeding' in which those who receive the sacrament in faith feed on Christ spiritually. This doctrine which was spoken of as 'double eating' Cranmer had learned from Martin Bucer, who taught 'we confess two things to be in the sacrament; an earthly, viz., bread and wine, which remain unchanged: and a heavenly, Christ our Lord himself who does not leave heaven...but gives himself in a heavenly manner for the food and sustenance of eternal life'.[1] Charles Smyth commented, 'For Bucer, Christ is not merely signified, but...eaten by faith in the power of the Spirit'.[2] Article 28 *Of the Lord's Supper*, underlines this fact that to receive the sacrament 'rightly and worthily' means with faith.

In both the 1552 and 1662 liturgies Cranmer repeatedly refers to the Eucharist as 'a feast of *spiritual* food'. At the end of the first exhortation in the 1552 order, which is to be said when the curate sees people 'negligent to come to the Holy Communion', Cranmer speaks of it as 'the banquet of the most heavenly food'. At the beginning of the Second Exhortation in the 1552 book, the Communion is spoken of as 'our *spiritual* food' though this phrase was removed by the compilers of the 1662 book. The third exhortation in both the 1552 and the 1662 books inform us that 'the benefit is great when 'we *spiritually* eat the flesh of Christ, and drink his blood; then we dwell in Christ, and Christ in us'.

5.1. Nourishment through faith.

In his *Defence* Cranmer laid great stress on this concept of *spiritual* eating. 'Christ's body and blood', he wrote, 'are not received in the mouth, and digested in the stomach, (as corporal meats and drinks

---

[1] Smyth, *Cranmer and the Reformation under Edward VI*, p 167.
[2] Smyth, *Cranmer and the Reformation under Edward VI*, p 168.

commonly be) but is received with a pure heart and a sincere faith'.[3] At the start of the Third Book of his *Defence* in the section entitled, 'the manner how Christ is present in his Supper', he draws the contrast between the Papists who 'teach that Christ is in the bread and wine' and his fellow Protestants who say that 'he is in them that worthily drink the bread and wine'.[4] Later in another paragraph in the Fourth Book Cranmer repeats the point. He begins by referring to the words of Chrysostom that in speaking of 'very flesh and blood' Jesus was using 'figurative speech' and that the bread and wine be 'signs, figures, and tokens instituted by him 'to represent unto us his very flesh and blood'. Then he continues, 'And yet as with our corporal eyes, corporal hands, and mouths, we do corporally see, feel, taste and eat the bread and drink the wine, being signs and sacraments of Christ's body, even so with our spiritual eyes, hands, and mouths, we do spiritually see, feel, taste, and eat his very flesh and drink his very blood'.[5]

5.2. Consecration by eating and drinking in faith,

Cranmer recognised that the major issue was who or what consecrated the bread and wine? Was it the priest reciting Jesus' words of institution over the bread and wine, or was it the manual acts of the priest laying his hands on the paten and the chalice, or was it the calling down of the Holy Spirit (epiclesis) on them to change them into the body and blood of Christ? With the passing of time it was clear that Cranmer did not hold to any of those views. He was clear that 'consecration is the separation of any thing from a profane and worldly use unto a spiritual use'.[6] Indeed to make the point explicit Cranmer removed the words 'consecrate', 'bless' and 'sanctify' from the 1552 liturgy. He pointed out that in baptism ordinary water is taken from other ordinary uses, and put to use for baptism. In the same way 'ordinary bread and wine is taken and severed from other bread and wine, to the use of Holy Communion' although it remains the same substance as that from which it was

---

[3] *Defence*, Bk 1, Ch, 16, p 74.
[4] *Defence*, Bk 3, Ch 2, p 124.
[5] *Defence*, Bk 4, Ch 8, p 209.
[6] *Defence*, Bk 3, Ch 15, p 181.

severed.[7] Cranmer went on to argue in this same section that 'the bread and wine have no holiness in them'.[8] It is for this reason that the sacrament is not to 'be worshipped and adored, as the papists term it, which is plainly idolatry'.[9] Cranmer made this explicitly clear in *Article 25* which stated, 'The sacraments were not ordained of Christ to be gazed upon, or carried about, but that we should duly use them'. This article which drew on the Augsburg Confession goes on to state: 'and in such only as worthily receive the same they have a wholesome effect or operation: but they that receive them unworthily purchase to themselves damnation as St Paul saith'.[10] For Cranmer, worthily receiving the bread and wine meant eating and drinking, trusting in Christ for forgiveness and in remembrance of his death and passion.

The Roman church's view was that good Christian men and women only eat the body and blood 'at that time when they receive the sacrament'. In contrast, Cranmer held strongly to the view that people can eat, drink and feed on Christ 'continually, so long as they are members of his body'.[11] Cranmer did not believe there was a single moment when the bread and wine were consecrated and so became the body and blood of Christ. It was for this reason that in the 1552 consecration prayer there was no epiclesis or calling down the Holy Spirit on the bread and wine. Nor was the priest required to engage in any manual act by laying his hands on the cup or the paten as later became the case in the 1662 Communion liturgy.

What enabled a person to receive the spiritual presence of Christ into their lives was simply eating and drinking with faith in him. The only point in Cranmer's 1552 consecration prayer where it is suggested that the communicants may be 'partakers of the body and blood of Christ' is as they are 'receiving these thy creatures of bread and wine, according to thy son our saviour Jesus Christ's holy institution'. In the communion therefore, Jesus' body and blood are received but only in a heavenly and spiritual manner, and that as the

---

[7] *Defence*, Bk 3, Ch 15, p 181.
[8] *Defence*, Bk 3, Ch 15, p 181.
[9] *Defence*, Bk 3, Ch 15, p 191.
[10] See C. Neil and J.M. Willoughby, *The Tutorial Prayer Book* (London, Church Book Room Press Ltd, 1959) pp 561-562.
[11] *Defence*, Bk 3, Ch 2, p 125.

communicants eat and drink in faith. This is made plain by Cranmer's 1552 words of distribution as the bread is given to each communicant: 'take and eat this...and *feed on him* [not in the mouth but] *in thy heart* with thanksgiving'. Cranmer is clear that this spiritual feeding need not and should not end in the Communion service. Rather, Christians should be those who feed continually on the presence of Christ. Holy Communion should both encourage and assist the believer to grow in this practice.

To sum up, in the 1552 communion there is nowhere any suggestion that the bread and wine change in substance. However in the 1662 revision of Cranmer's service we do find the re-introduction of the manual acts of the 1549 liturgy where the minister is instructed to place his hand over the paten and the chalice suggesting a moment of change. By the same token Cranmer is also clear that it is not the minister or priest who consecrates bread and wine but it is the communicants rightly receiving them who do so, as they eat and drink in faith and in consequence feed on the spiritual presence of Christ. If we can accept Cranmer's view that by eating and drinking with faith and love for Christ each communicant consecrates the bread and wine, it makes the concept of lay presidency a logical one. It is doubtful however that such an idea would ever have entered Cranmer's mind. Nevertheless it is clear that in early times the New Passover, like its Jewish predecessor, was celebrated in small groups or family gatherings in the home with only a lay person presiding.

In the third book of his *Defence* which Cranmer devotes to the Presence of Christ in the sacrament, he sets out a number of reasons why there can be no substantial or bodily presence of Christ in the consecrated bread and wine. He cites several passages from the gospels in support of this, beginning with John 15 where Jesus says, 'I leave the world and go to my Father'. He then makes reference to Jesus' words in Matthew 26 that 'You shall ever have poor folk with you, but you shall not ever have me with you'.[12] He points out from Mark 16 that Jesus was taken up into heaven, and sitteth on the right hand of the throne of God's majesty'. He also adds to quotations from the Letter to the Hebrews 'that we have a High Priest that sitteth in

---

[12] *Defence*, Bk 3, ch 4, p 128 citing Matthew 26.11

heaven at the right hand of the throne of God's majesty'.[13] In keeping with his usual method, Cranmer then supports his theme with references taken from the Early Church Fathers. 'Origen', he writes, 'hath plainly declared his mind, that Christ's body is not both present here with us, and also gone hence and estranged from us'.[14] Likewise he quotes Augustine that 'As concerning the presence of his Majesty, we have Christ ever with us; but as concerning the presence of his flesh, he said truly to his disciples, Ye shall not ever have me with you'.[15] Similarly he takes support from the words of Ambrose, 'That we must not seek Christ upon earth, nor in earth, but in heaven, where he sitteth at the right hand of his Father', and of Gregory that 'Christ is not here by the presence of his flesh, and yet he is absent no where by the presence of his majesty'.[16] He then adds a brief quotation from Epiphanius who stated that 'Christ speaking of a loaf which is round in fashion, and cannot see, hear, nor feel, said of it, This is my body'.[17]

Cranmer stresses this point that communicants feed only on material bread and wine and receive only a spiritual presence of Christ as they do so. He cites Origen, Tertullian and Chrysostom and several other Early Church Fathers who understood Jesus' words about eating and drinking his body and blood only in a spiritual sense. 'Consider that these things', wrote Origen, 'are figures; and therefore examine and understand them, as spiritual and not carnal men'.[18] Chrysostom wrote similarly, 'Christ ordained the table of his holy supper for this purpose, that in the sacrament he should daily show unto us bread and wine in the similitude of his body and blood'.[19] For good measure Cranmer also quotes from Ambrose's *Concerning the Sacraments* where he stated, 'As thou hast in baptism received the similitude of death, so likewise dost thou in this sacrament drink the similitude of Christ's precious blood'. Cranmer eventually sums up this matter by pointing out that 'Christ himself

---

[13] *Defence*, Bk 3, Ch 4, p 128. He also cites Colossians 3:1 'Set your hearts on things above where Christ is seated at the right hand of God'.
[14] *Defence*, Bk 3, Ch 5, p129.
[15] *Defence*, Bk 3, Ch 5, p130.
[16] *Defence*, Bk 3, Ch 5, p 132.
[17] *Defence*, Bk 3, Ch 7, p 142.
[18] *Defence*, Bk 3, Ch10, p 147.
[19] *Defence*, Bk 3, Ch 11, p 151.

often speaks in similitudes, parables, and figures',[20] obvious examples being his discourse on the vine, the bread of life, the good shepherd and the door.

5.3. Nourishment from the word of God, teaching and preaching.

Cranmer wrote in his Catechism that we can do 'no greater works' on the Sabbath-day than 'to hear the word of God' and prepare ourselves that we may worthily be partakers of the Lord's table. Thereby we receive 'great comfort, to the quiet of our consciences and confirmation of our faith'.[21] In this statement it is clear that Cranmer saw that preaching and teaching from the Bible went hand in hand with the sacrament of the Lord's Supper. The expounding of Scripture was indeed both a preparation for the feast and also added to the spiritual food which the congregation receive. In other words the worshippers would feed by faith on the spiritual presence of Christ the Bread of Life and on the truths of God's word. The fact that Cranmer saw the expounding of Scripture as a key part of this spiritual feeding is borne out in the Collect for the Second Sunday in Advent which he originally wrote for the 1549 Prayer Book:

> Blessed Lord, who has caused all holy scriptures to be written for our learning; Grant that we may in such wise hear them, read, mark, learn and inwardly digest them, that by patience and comfort of thy holy word, we may embrace and ever hold fast the blessed hope of everlasting life, which thou hast given us in our Saviour Jesus Christ.

The key words of Cranmer's prayer in this are 'inwardly digest' which remind us that we are fed, nourished and sustained by God's word.

5.4. Sermons provide additional spiritual food.

For this reason Cranmer made provision for a sermon and a reading from an epistle and gospel at each service. He had no place for priests

---

[20] *Defence*, Bk 3, Ch 11, p 164.
[21] T. Cranmer, *Catechism* in *Writings of the Rev. Dr Thomas Cranmer* (London, The Religious Tract Society, undated) p 129.

'as pretend to be Christ's successors in making a sacrifice to him...for no person made a sacrifice of Christ, but he himself only'.[22] Cranmer did not believe Christian ministers had any priestly, sacrificial role. Their function was to be a preacher and teacher of Scripture, to pastor the people and to minister the bread and wine of Communion. This fact was made abundantly clear in the ordination services of both the 1552 and the 1662 *Prayer Books*. Those who were made deacon received a New Testament from the bishop with the words, 'Take thou authority to read the Gospel in the Church of God, and to preach the same'. Similarly priests received a copy of the Bible with the words, 'Take thou authority to preach the word of God, and to minister the holy sacraments in this congregation where thou shalt be appointed'. In the 1552 Communion provision was made for a sermon immediately following the creed. If the minister was either not licensed by the bishop to preach, or if he was, but had not prepared a sermon, he was required to read one from the *Book of Homilies* which had been published in 1547. Significantly, the first sermon in the book was written by Cranmer and entitled, 'A Fruitful Reading of Holy Scripture'. Other titles included, 'On the Salvation of all Mankind', 'Of the true and lively faith', 'Of Good Works' and 'An exhortation against the Fear of Death'.

Cranmer did not believe the priest or minister to be in any way ontologically different from the laity. He certainly did not subscribe to any notion of the spirit of the apostles being passed down to or residing in the clergy by virtue of their ordination. He was adamant that the bishop's hands made no such change. 'The difference between the priest and the layman in this matter', he wrote, 'is only in the ministration; that the priest as the common minister of the Church, doth minister and distribute the Lord's Supper unto other, and the other receive it at his hands'.[23]

In the Communion service therefore Cranmer held the minister's core roles and duties were to be to ensure that the Scriptures (a passage from a New Testament letter and a passage from a Gospel) were read, a sermon given and the bread and wine administered to the people. As has been noted, Cranmer did not

---

[22] *Defence*, Bk 5, Ch 5, p 220.
[23] *Defence*, Bk 5, Ch 11, p 224.

believe there was a moment of consecration when the priest caused a change to take place in either the nature or status of the bread and wine. His view was quite simply that the bread and wine were consecrated by the communicants rightly receiving and feeding on them in their hearts by faith. Christ, as Cranmer understood it, 'instituted and gave the Supper to the whole church' and the priest's function was therefore quite simply that of a servant bringing food to the table at a meal, or to put it in his own words 'to minister and distribute the elements ... to all that would duly ask for it'.[24]

5.5. 'All other benefits of his passion'.

The first post-communion prayer contains the following petition, 'that we and all thy whole church may obtain remission of our sins, and *all other benefits of his passion*'. A little later there follows a further request that 'all we which be partakers of this Holy Communion, *may be fulfilled with thy grace and heavenly benediction*'. Both these two prayers make mention of the benefits which believers can and should derive from Holy Communion and yet they are often largely ignored or passed over altogether in contemporary Holy Communion services. Yet this was a matter which was clearly central in Cranmer's understanding of the sacrament.

When a person dies there are benefits accruing from their will. When Jesus died he brought lasting forgiveness through his death on the cross which was 'a full, perfect, and sufficient sacrifice, oblation and satisfaction, for the sins of the whole world'. It is this forgiveness that the communicants receive and remember by eating and drinking the bread and wine. In addition, by his death Jesus bestowed other benefits. The New Testament is clear that he brought peace through the blood of his cross. Peter's first letter reminds us that by Jesus' wounds we have been healed (1 Peter 2:24). The author of the Letter to the Hebrews tells us that through his death Jesus is able to cleanse our consciences from guilt (Hebrews 9:14). In addition to this the prophet Isaiah foresaw that in his death Jesus would bear his followers' griefs and carry their sorrows (Isaiah 53:4). It is these and other spiritual benefits that Cranmer believed the

---

[24] *Defence*, Bk 5, Ch 11, p 224.

congregation should be receiving from the Lord as they feed on Christ's presence by faith as they eat the bread and drink the wine. Cranmer urges this in his Catechism, which states that 'on such days [at the Lord's Table] chiefly we ought in faith and spirit fervently to pray to God, to give us all good things that we lack and have need of, and to defend and deliver us from all evil things'.[25]

---

[25] T. Cranmer, *Catechism* in *Writings of Thomas Cranmer*, p 129.

6. A Meal for Remembrance.

6.1. *The New Passover.*

Cranmer is mindful of Jesus' words that the Lord's Supper is the New Passover Meal. All three of the synoptic gospels set the institution of the Lord's Supper in the context of the Passover (Matthew 26:18-19 and Mark 14:12) and Luke records Jesus' words to his disciples 'With desire I have desired to eat this Passover Meal with you' (Luke 22:15). John's Gospel sets the Eucharist in the context of the feeding of the five thousand (John 6:53-59) and significantly mentions that the Jewish feast of the Passover was near (John 6:4). Cranmer reminds his readers that 'the pure paschal lamb without spot, signified Christ' and that 'the effusion of the lamb's blood, signified the effusion of Christ's blood'. He continues the theme, 'And the salvation of the children of Israel from temporal death by the lamb's blood, signified our salvation from eternal death by Christ's blood'.[1] He develops the parallelism with the Passover at some length, further reminding his readers that as 'he [the angel of death] passed by the children of Israel's houses where he saw the lamb's blood upon the doors, and hurted none of them,...so likewise at the last judgement of the whole world, none shall be passed over and saved, but that shall be found marked by the blood of the most pure and immaculate lamb Jesus Christ'.[2] Cranmer summed up the links between the Passover and the Lord's Supper in the following paragraph.

> For as much as this holy bread broken, the wine divided do represent unto us the death of Christ now passed, as the killing of the Paschal lamb do represent unto us the death of Christ now passed, as the killing of the Paschal lamb did represent the same yet to come: therefore our Saviour Christ used the same figure of speech of the bread and wine, as God used of the Paschal lamb. For as in the Old Testament God said, *This is the Lord's pass-by, or Passover*, even so saith Christ in the New Testament, *This is my body, This is my blood*. But in

---

[1] *Defence*, Bk 3, Ch 12, p 165.
[2] *Defence*, Bk 3, Ch 12, p 165.

the old mystery and sacrament, the lamb was not the Lord's very Passover or passing-by, but it was a figure which represented his passing by. So like wise in the New Testament the bread and wine be not Christ's very body and blood, but they be figures, which by Christ's institution be unto the godly receivers thereof sacraments, tokens, significations, and representations of his very flesh and blood.[3]

Just as in the Passover the Old Testament believers remembered their deliverance from bondage and slavery in Egypt on account of the blood smeared on the door posts of their houses, so in the Lord's Supper Christians are called to remember their deliverance from slavery to their sin and selfishness. Both the Passover and the Lord's Supper were intended to be a vivid remembrance or recalling of the past so that it lives in their present thoughts and hearts. Throughout the 1552 liturgy Cranmer calls the communicants to this kind of remembrance as an important part of their spirituality.

6.2. Remembrance in the Communion liturgies

In the third exhortation in both the 1552 and 1662 liturgies the priest charges the congregation that they 'should always *remember* the exceeding great love of our Master, and only Saviour Jesus Christ, thus dying for us'. The consecration prayer calls the people not in any way to offer the bread and wine but to receive the bread and wine 'in *remembrance* of his (Christ's) death and passion'. The words which were then spoken as the administration of the bread and wine in the 1552 rite were words of thanksgiving in remembrance of Jesus' death and passion.

The words spoken during the administration in the 1549 rite were, 'The body of our Lord Jesus Christ preserve thy body and soul unto everlasting life' and 'The blood of our Lord Jesus Christ preserve thy body and soul unto everlasting life'. When the 1549 book came into use a number clergy were of the view that it was still possible to use it and retain a belief in the doctrine of transubstantiation.

---

[3] *Defence*, Bk 3, Ch 12, p 166.

Following advice from Bucer and others Cranmer changed the wording to, 'Take and eat this, in *remembrance* that Christ died for thee, and feed on him in thy heart and be thankful' and 'Drink this in *remembrance* that Christ's blood was shed for thee, and be thankful'. When Queen Elizabeth I came to the throne and re-introduced worship in English she combined the 1549 words of administration with those of the 1552. In consequence her *Prayer Book* of 1559 which was almost entirely based on the 1552 *Prayer Book*, hinted at a compromise over the presence of Christ in the elements. In fact Elizabeth herself is reported to have quoted a verse from the poet John Donne which suggests exactly that.

> His was the words that spake it.
> He took the bread and brake it
> And what his word doth make it
> That I believe and take it.[4]

All of this makes it clear that Cranmer was seeking to bring the Lord's Supper much more into line with the practice of the early church. Whilst he was possibly content that Holy Communion could be a central Sunday service in his own society which was after all a Christendom in which all citizens were at least nominally Christians, it is less likely that he would have countenanced the practice in our contemporary secular culture. There are always those who argue that the Lord's Supper is 'a converting ordinance' but Cranmer was too well aware of the practice of the early Christian churches of the second and third centuries to buy into that argument. It was not generally anticipated at that time in the church's history that those who were un-baptised would be present at the Lord's Supper which was regarded solely as the worship of the people of God. *The Didache*, which some scholars date as early as AD 100 and which can be considered the first service book of the early church, lays down the following instruction, 'Let no one eat or drink of your Eucharist except those baptised into the name of the Lord; for, as regards this, the Lord has said, "Give not that which is holy unto dogs"'. The *Apostolic Constitutions*, a fourth century collection of church laws, lays it down that at the beginning of the Lord's Supper the deacon shall say, 'Let none of the catechumens (those still under instruction), let

---

[4] J. Donne, 'On the Sacrament', *Divine Poems*.

none of the hearers (that is those who had come to the service because they were interested in Christianity), let none of the unbelievers, let none of the heretics, stay here'. Theodoret (c393-c457) the Church historian and Bishop of Cyrrhus in Syria, quotes what he says is an unwritten saying of Jesus, 'My mysteries are for myself and for my people'.

As has been already been noted scholars such as Joachim Jeremias and others have demonstrated that the Lord's Supper is the continuation of the Passover feast and although it was, and is still, intended to be an interactive informal joyous occasion in the home, it was nevertheless restricted to those who were God's people. According to the Book of Exodus, no temporary resident, hired worker, foreigner or uncircumcised male was allowed to celebrate the Passover.[5] If the church can recognise the Holy Communion as the 'New Passover' and return to this early Christian practice of home-based worship for the believing community, it follows that it will not be necessary to make Holy Communion the weekly main or central Sunday service. The Lord's Supper was never designed or intended for the uncommitted or the unbeliever to dip into. Cranmer was clear that it was only for those who could 'truly and earnestly repent of their sins' and 'draw near' and 'receive the holy sacrament for their comfort'. He summed the matter up in the following lines in his *Defence*, 'Wherefore in this sacrament (if it be rightly **received** with a true faith) we be assured that our sins be forgiven,...so that whosoever by a true faith doth eat Christ's flesh and drink his blood, hath everlasting life by him. Which thing when we feel in our hearts at **the receiving** of the Lord's Supper, what thing can be more joyful, more pleasant, or more comfortable to us'.[6] If the words of Archbishop William Temple are taken seriously that 'the Church is the only society on earth that exists for the benefit of non-members', local churches would be offering something on Sundays so that those who are strangers to the Christian faith can come and look into our worship without finding anything strange, uncomfortable or esoteric.

---

[5] Exodus 12:43-49.
[6] *Defence*, Bk 1, Ch 16, p76.

7. A Meal for Thanksgiving.

Central to the Eucharist, as the very name implies, is thanksgiving – the Greek word *eucharisto* meaning 'to give thanks'. This key aspect is abundantly clear in Jesus' words of institution. Having taken the cup at the Last Supper, he gave *thanks*. This same note of thanksgiving was characteristic of both Jewish prayers and Jewish fellowship meals. For example, before the feeding of the five thousand and indeed the four thousand, Jesus took the bread and the fish and gave thanks and then distributed the food to the hungry crowds. Cranmer had long wanted to remove from the Communion service any suggestion that it was a sacrifice for the sins of the people. It was at this point that he decided to replace the sacrifice made by the priest at the altar, as in the Mass, with a sacrifice of praise made by the people. The Letter to the Hebrews endorsed exactly this change pointing out that the animal sacrifices made by the priests in the temple were no longer in force but there was another kind sacrifice which is very necessary, the sacrifice of praise and thanksgiving (Hebrews 13:15).

7.1. A sacrifice of thanksgiving

The central focus of the Medieval Mass (whether the Bangor, York, Hereford or Sarum rite) was the offering up by the priest of the transubstantiated elements for the sins of the living and the dead. In the Sarum Mass for example, the priest prayed: 'Therefore, Lord, we beseech thee that thou, being pacified, wilt receive this oblation of our bound service and of all thy household' and again, 'Wherefore, O Lord, we...do offer unto thy excellent majesty of thy own rewards and gifts + a pure host, + a holy host, + an undefiled host, the holy + bread of eternal life, and + cup of eternal salvation'. After the reception the priest prayed 'Lord, let this communion purge us from sin, and make us to be partakers of the heavenly remedy'. In place of this 'sacrificial offering of the body and blood of Christ', Cranmer substituted 'a sacrificial offering of praise and thanksgiving'. Here once again Cranmer the biblical scholar drew on the Hebrews passage which makes it clear that there is no propitiatory sacrifice that can offered since 'the one only perfect sacrifice and satisfaction for the sins of the whole world' has already been offered (Hebrews

10:14). The Apostle then goes on to make the following exhortation: 'Through Jesus, therefore, let us continually offer to God a *sacrifice of praise* – the fruit of lips that confess his name'(Hebrews 13:15). Cranmer made this emphasis on the need for praise and thanksgiving very clearly at the beginning of chapter 3 of the *Defence:*

> Another kind of sacrifice there is, which doth not reconcile us to God, but is made of them that be reconciled by Christ, to testify our duties unto God, and to show ourselves thankful unto him: and therefore they be called sacrifices of laud, praise and thanksgiving. The first kind of sacrifice Christ offered to God for us; the second kind we ourselves offer to God by Christ. And by the first kind of sacrifice Christ offered also for us unto his Father; and the second we offer ourselves and all that we have, unto his Father.[1]

Cranmer included a number of passages in his *Defence* which underline the importance of thanksgiving as an integral part of the Lord's Supper. At the beginning of chapter 12 of the fifth book he noted that the prophet Malachi foresaw that everywhere all faithful people would bring to God not 'any oblation propitiatory to be made by the priests', but rather 'in what place soever [sic] they be with pure hearts and minds, sacrifices of laud and praise'.[2] In another paragraph in the following chapter Cranmer wrote that the Supper was ordained 'that every man eating and drinking thereof should remember that Christ died for him...and so give unto Christ most hearty thanks, and give himself also clearly unto him'.[3] After briefly surveying the writers of the early Christian church he concluded that 'when the old fathers called the mass, or Supper of the Lord, a sacrifice, they meant that it was a sacrifice of lauds and thanksgiving'.[4]

7.2. *Thanksgiving for our redemption and all the blessings of life.*

These two aspects of thanksgiving are the focus of Cranmer's concern for thankfulness in the context of the Eucharist. Cranmer would

---

[1] *Defence*, Bk 5, Ch 3, p 217.
[2] *Defence*, Bk 5, Ch 12, p 225.
[3] *Defence*, Bk 5, Ch 13, p 227.
[4] *Defence*, Bk 5, Ch 16, p 229.

certainly have agreed with the great Victorian Baptist preacher, Charles Spurgeon, who once wrote that 'thanksgiving is all we can give to God and the least we can give'. In the same paragraph Spurgeon continued, 'Let us be at all times thoroughly fervent...both with our lips and with our lives, by thanksgiving and thanksliving'.[5] When Cranmer produced his second *Prayer Book* in 1552 he therefore set both the Prayer of Thanksgiving and the Gloria after the consecration and reception of the bread and wine. In this way, which is followed by the 1662 service, communicants are reminded of the importance of giving praise and thanksgiving to the Lord, supremely for the gift of salvation but also for 'all other benefits of his Passion'. The Prayer of Thanksgiving begins, 'O Lord and heavenly father, we thy humble servants entirely desire thy fatherly goodness, mercifully to accept this our sacrifice of praise and thanksgiving'. In the Gloria the worshippers declare, 'We praise thee, we bless thee, we worship thee, we glorify thee, we give thanks to thee for thy great glory, O Lord God heavenly king, God the Father Almighty'. Cranmer's pattern clearly resonates with the gospels of Matthew and Mark which both record that at the conclusion of the Last Supper the disciples sang a hymn presumably of thanks and praise to God.[6] Significantly, the Collect or prayer for cleansing at the commencement of both the 1552 and the 1662 orders focuses the attention of the worshippers on the importance of praise and worship as the congregation are invited to pray that 'we may perfectly love thee, and worthily magnify thy holy name through Christ our Lord'.

7.3. Thanksgiving often lacking in contemporary Holy Communion services.

Although this note of thanksgiving is clearly apparent in Cranmer's order for Communion, such thanks is often lacking in additional intercessions offered by the service leader or other persons in most forms of contemporary public worship and in Communion in particular. Cranmer's liturgy draws our attention to the fact that thanksgiving is a marked characteristic both in the life of Jesus and in

---

[5] C.H. Spurgeon, *The Treasury of David* (New York. Funk and Wagnalls, 1882) commentary on Psalm 107 verse 1.
[6] Matthew 26:30 and Mark 14:26.

the early Christian communities. In the worship of the Jerusalem temple thanksgiving was regarded as the way into the presence of God.[7] Again the writer of the Letter to the Hebrews urges that 'since we are receiving a kingdom that cannot be shaken, let us be thankful, and so worship God acceptably with reverence and awe.' (Hebrews 12:28). This note of gratitude also finds echoes in Paul's letters to the Ephesians and the Colossians.[8] Perhaps it should be noted that a lack of thanksgiving is a mark of the unregenerate.[9] In summary it is the case that the sacrament of Holy Communion is a service of thanksgiving from beginning to end!

---

[7] See for example Psalm 95:2; Psalm 100:4.
[8] Ephesians 5:20; Colossians 3:16.
[9] Romans 1:21; 1 Timothy 3:2.

8. Cranmer's understanding of the Lord's Supper for Today.

If Cranmer was indeed a work in progress, as Michael Davis, Colin Buchanan[1] and others have asserted and with good reason, he would surely have gone on to incorporate further changes to liturgy of the Lord' Supper. These would have been in a Protestant direction based on his understanding of the teaching of Scripture rather than the minor reversals made in the opposite directions by the Restoration church in 1662 and the more blatant departures from Scripture expressed in some parts of the more recent Communion liturgies of *Common Worship*. Among the implications of Cranmer's understanding of the Lord's Supper for the contemporary church are some of the following.

8.1. Not an optional Extra.

It is too easy for Communion to slip into becoming a short early morning version or a 'tacked-on' optional extra at the end of the morning or evening worship. Against such practice Cranmer stresses on believers the importance of coming to the Lord's table. In the exhortation immediately following the prayer for the Church Militant, the Curate is to urge the people 'for the Lord Jesus Christ's sake ... not to refuse to come to Lord's Supper'. In what follows an illustration is given of a man who prepared a rich feast with every kind of food and which lacked for nothing apart from guests. 'Which of you in such a case', the exhortation goes on to ask, 'would not think a great injury and wrong be done unto him'? In a similar way Christian men and women need to beware lest they likewise 'provoke God's indignation by refusing to come to the Lord's table'. Drawing on Jesus' parable of the Great Supper Party where the invited guests excuse their attendance at the feast on grounds of business, work and marriage, the Curate goes on to exhort the congregants 'to love their own salvation' and to be partakers of the Lord's Supper. Such laxity

---

[1] Buchanan, *What did Cranmer Think he was Doing?*, p 9; Davies, *Cranmer's Godly Order*, p 56 and 91. See also D. Stone, *The Book of Common Prayer in the Church of England; its making and revisions, 1549-1561* (London, 1949) p 15.

does 'great injury to God', and causes a separation from those Christian men and women who do attend. The slightly longer 1552 version includes the memorable sentence that 'ye offend God so sore in refusing this holy banquet'.

8.2. Sunday worship

If we return to the early church practice and encourage home-based Holy Communion, it follows that it will not be necessary to make the sacrament a main or central Sunday service. In the reign of Elizabeth I, Morning Prayer was the main order of the day and Communion services were separate occasions for the more seriously committed Christians of the parish. Indeed, attendance was only compulsory at Easter and even then excuses could be found.[2] If we really want to reach out to those who are total strangers to the Christian faith we should be offering something on Sundays that avoids the strange, the uncomfortable or the esoteric. Cranmer was plainly aware that even in the nominal medieval Christendom of the Middle Ages, having Mass as the central service was hardly justifiable for this very reason. In any event, it seems clear in the present era that the nation's largest and expanding churches are by and large those which avoid having Communion as their main or central Sunday service. Parish churches therefore need expressions of worship which are relaxed, visitor and stranger friendly, and yet at the same time are applied and relevant to the business of everyday living and the work place. It needs to be visual, to have spiritual vitality and in the words of John Wesley, to convey 'the plain truth to the plain man'.

The question then presents itself how and when should Holy Communion be held in our main church building? Clearly if there is already an established early morning service it may be best to retain it. In addition, assuming that small groups and families are breaking bread in homes, it might be good to encourage the whole congregation to come together on one Sunday evening in the month, or on a chosen week-night, to share in the Lord's Supper. Such occasions need to be informal in style, avoiding the ethos of the local Bach choral society, not rigidly liturgical and without clerical dress,

---

[2] E. Ives, *The Reformation Experience*, (Abingdon, Lion Hudson, 2012) p 249.

bearing in mind that the use of ciboria, cruets, lavabo jugs, thuribles, incense boats and spoons, burses, purificators, corporals, mass gongs and other items which have perhaps unkindly been dubbed 'eucharistic toys' need to be avoided at all costs. Hopefully on such occasions it will be possible to emphasise the corporate nature of the sacrament with all the participants eating the bread together rather than each worshipper doing it separately, followed by the taking the wine. From time to time there may be some real value in separating the sharing of the bread from the sharing of the wine by a longer period as in the Lukan and Pauline tradition. On occasion, there may also be significant benefits in allowing the participants to pass the consecrated bread and wine to one another in the manner of Luke 22:17 where Jesus took the cup and told the disciples 'to share it among themselves'.

8.3. Greater emphasis on teaching and biblical exposition

It is often the case, and particularly so in the case of early morning Communion services, that insufficient time and attention are given to biblical teaching and preaching. Cranmer made clear provision in the rubric following the creed, which is found in both the 1552 and 1662 service books, that 'there should follow the Sermon, or one of the homilies'. The homilies are substantial doctrinal and biblical expositions of Scripture, a fact which makes it obvious that Cranmer would not have countenanced 'the short address' or the mere commenting on the epistle and gospel of the day. For Cranmer the word and sacrament go hand in hand, with the exposition of Scripture forming an important part of the spiritual feeding by faith. As Gerard Hughes put it, 'The word of God is a special sacrament of his presence, just as real, although different in form, as his presence in the Eucharist'.[3] Cranmer clearly anticipated that the priest or presbyter would take their teaching role with great seriousness and would faithfully teach and expound the Scriptures in such a way that Christ's very presence would be imparted into the hearts of those who listened. His collect for the Second Sunday in Advent succinctly expresses his aspiration in the matter:

---

[3] G. Hughes, *The God of Surprises* (London, Darton, Longman and Todd, 1985) p 46.

Blessed Lord, who has caused all holy Scriptures to be written for our learning: Grant that we may in such wise hear them, read, mark, learn and inwardly digest them, that by patience of thy Holy Word, we may embrace and ever hold fast the blessed hope of everlasting life, which thou hast given us in our Saviour Jesus Christ, Amen.[4]

8.4. Taking note of Cranmer's understanding of consecration

Cranmer's understanding of consecration points forward to the rightness of lay celebration. Cranmer, as has been noted, was clear that there was no one specific moment of consecration of the bread and wine. The bread and wine were consecrated or set apart for holy use as each believer ate and drank with faith and trust in Christ, remembering his death and passion. If this is accepted then it becomes clear as Cranmer himself saw that the priest or minister is simply the duly appointed official who serves at the table. He or she is in no way ontologically different by virtue of having received an ordination at the bishop's hands. Cranmer was totally clear on this point.

It is plain enough that Cranmer was of course seeking to rid the newly formed Church of England of the priest as a mystery 'hocus pocus'[5] man who could turn bread into God at the altar. It is also clear that had Cranmer been alive at the present time he would probably not have been happy with the role played by many contemporary clergy in their officiating role at Communion services. Even numbers of those who align themselves with the evangelical section of the church have departed from Cranmer's rubric for unobtrusive and plain clerical garb and appear at the communion table clad in albs

---

[4] Collect for The Second Sunday in Advent.
[5] 'Hocus pocus' is derived from the Latin '*Hoc est corpus meum*' meaning 'This is my body', the words recited by the priest when consecrating the bread.

and stoles.⁶ Such vesture hardly bespeaks the humility and servant role of Jesus who concluded the Last Supper by washing the disciples' feet. The contemporary church needs to take note of the fact (as Dom Gregory Dix pointed out in his major study *The Shape of the Liturgy*), that no special vestments were worn until the later years of Constantine's rule.⁷ Perhaps the most appropriate clerical garb for today's clergy leading a Communion service is some form of smart casual attire.

Too many of to-day's clergy still sit in state on the big seats at the front of the church building clad in the dress of a first century Roman citizen awaiting for the gradual hymn to end so that they can begin their 'Sunday preside' or celebrant role. This does not always help to give the sense of the whole family of God gathering together as brothers and sisters, Cranmerian style, round the family table to share the family meal. Furthermore such an environment is not ideal for the majority of occasional visitors, let alone to those who are strangers to the Christian faith, and decide on one occasion in a year to darken a church door. People who drop into their local parish church the Sunday following a family bereavement or after a positive experience at an *Alpha* or *Christianity Explored* course are not going to feel comfortable in such situations. We may note at this point Jesus' warnings against both robes and big seats (Luke 20:46; Matthew 23:6). Lengthy theological recitations from a heavy black volume of some 850 pages or even the red slimmed-down version that begins on page 158 can be an unnerving prospect for newcomers, while processions of cups, candles, plates and wafers may seem strange, odd or unnecessary. Those who have experienced a public school chapel may well of course have some understanding of what Archbishop Cranmer aptly described as 'these holy mysteries' but the great majority of British citizens will probably find it a struggle.

---

[6] It should be note that albs were the every-day dress of the average Roman citizen and the stole an indicator or badge of their rank or profession. When the pagan Goths and Vandals overran the city of Rome church leaders retained Roman dress as a way of showing their commitment to the Christian faith of the Empire. During the Middle Ages these garments became associated with the celebration of the Mass and invested with its theology. Cranmer and the Reformers therefore decided on plainer forms of dress.

[7] G. Dix, *The Shape of the Liturgy*, p 399.

8.5. More time for eating and drinking the bread and wine.

Cranmer was deeply impressed with the New Testament teaching that the Holy Communion is a 'supper' or in other words a meal. As is clear from the teaching of Paul and the gospel writers, the Lord's Supper was instituted at a meal. This practice of sharing Communion in the context of a meal or Agapé continued well into the second century in some parts of the Roman Empire.[8] William Barclay commented that 'it was a lovely custom; and it is to our loss that the custom has vanished. It was a way of producing and nourishing real Christian fellowship'.[9] Once separated from the shared meal, the sense of fellowship – and more importantly taking time to eat and drink the consecrated bread and wine and to deliberately and consciously receive spiritual nourishment – was largely lost.

This central act of Holy Communion, the eating and drinking of the bread and wine, has in most Anglican churches been reduced to a minute's kneeling at an altar rail or a few seconds standing in a lengthy cafeteria style queue where a priest or some other designated official clad in special robes thrusts a tiny piece of bread into their hands or pops a wafer between their lips which then gets stuck to the roof of their mouths. This is then followed by a step to the side to join the wine line for an equally quick and tiny sip from the cup. Clearly something needs to be done to bring the Eucharist more in line with the intention of Jesus and the practice of the early church. It is significant that in speaking of the Lord's Supper Paul uses the Greek word *deipnon*. In first century Greek society breakfast was a sparse affair which often consisted of a small portion of bread dipped in wine. The mid-day meal was also a light and generally casual affair often eaten in the street or the town square, but the supper was the main meal of the day. At the *deipnon* people sat down with no feeling of rush or hurry and then in a leisurely manner they ate and satisfied their hunger.

All this suggests that the Christian supper ought to be a meal where people relax, interact and enjoy one another's company. There should also be time to sit back, and in moments of quiet simply enjoy

---

[8] See pg26 footnotes 4-8.
[9] W. Barclay, *The Letters to the Corinthians* (Edinburgh, St Andrew Press, 1962) p 113.

the pleasure of being in the presence of God. Often communion liturgies are too lengthy and the clergy person leading feels under pressure to recite too much liturgy with insufficient time available before the children have to be collected from Sunday school or kids clubs. This makes the occasion one of rush and hurry. Clergy need constant reminding that the Lord most often speaks in a still small voice. Indeed we are often being reminded by the media that speed kills. A rushed world can do without a rushed church! The *Westminster Shorter Catechism* poses this question, 'What is man's chief end?', to which the answer is 'To worship God and enjoy him for ever'. We need time at Communion services to take this delight in the Lord's presence. After all, why would anyone want to rush through a good meal! All this suggests that it is preferable to receive the bread and wine seated rather than standing or kneeling. It is after all not normal to share a meal standing – let alone kneeling. In fact in his 1553 *Reformatio Legum Ecclesiasticarum* Cranmer did allow sitting.[10] Later when Elizabeth I re-introduced Cranmer's 1552 *Prayer Book* clergy administered the bread and wine to communicants, kneeling, sitting or standing as they thought fit.[11]

Central to this enjoyment of Christ's presence in an extended period for eating and drinking, is the time to truly remember and recall his love for each individual, which gives them self-acceptance, self-worth and confidence in their own identity. As we focus on the all sufficient cross which is so central to Cranmer's thinking, we are renewed in his love and in consequence strengthened in love and service of others.

By emphasising that the Communion is a meal and calling it 'The Lord's Supper' and also by stressing that it is a feast, Cranmer was demonstrating his awareness of the importance of eating and drinking thoughtfully, with faith and trust in Jesus, and with adequate opportunity to receive the nourishment of his Word and Spirit. If Colin Buchanan is correct in his contention that Cranmer was a work in progress, it seems probable that with the passing of time he would have made further adaptations and modifications to his Communion liturgy to provide adequate opportunity to enable the

---

[10] Buchanan, *What did Cranmer think He was Doing?*, p 29.
[11] Ives., *The Reformation Experience*, p 244. See also V.J.K. Brook, *A life of Archbishop Parker* (Oxford, Clarendon Press, 1962) p 167.

communicants to eat and drink in such a way as to receive spiritual nourishment and joyful interaction.

8.6. A final word

For Cranmer the Lord's Supper is the very heart of Christian worship. It is first and foremost a focus on the cross and the all sufficient death and resurrection of Christ through which alone salvation and eternal life are possible. It is the means by which each individual Christian believer is able to draw near and remain in close touch with Christ such that 'we might dwell in Him and He in us'. It is also, as Cranmer's own catechism reminds us, 'for the strengthening and refreshing of our souls'.

Latimer Publications

Latimer Studies

LS 01	The Evangelical Anglican Identity Problem	Jim Packer
LS 02	The ASB Rite A Communion: A Way Forward	Roger Beckwith
LS 03	The Doctrine of Justification in the Church of England	Robin Leaver
LS 04	Justification Today: The Roman Catholic and Anglican Debate	R. G. England
LS 05/06	Homosexuals in the Christian Fellowship	David Atkinson
LS 07	Nationhood: A Christian Perspective	O. R. Johnston
LS 08	Evangelical Anglican Identity: Problems and Prospects	Tom Wright
LS 09	Confessing the Faith in the Church of England Today	Roger Beckwith
LS 10	A Kind of Noah's Ark? The Anglican Commitment to Comprehensiveness	Jim Packer
LS 11	Sickness and Healing in the Church	Donald Allister
LS 12	Rome and Reformation Today: How Luther Speaks to the New Situation	James Atkinson
LS 13	Music as Preaching: Bach, Passions and Music in Worship	Robin Leaver
LS 14	Jesus Through Other Eyes: Christology in a Multi-faith Context	Christopher Lamb
LS 15	Church and State Under God	James Atkinson
LS 16	Language and Liturgy	Gerald Bray, Steve Wilcockson, Robin Leaver
LS 17	Christianity and Judaism: New Understanding, New Relationship	James Atkinson
LS 18	Sacraments and Ministry in Ecumenical Perspective	Gerald Bray
LS 19	The Functions of a National Church	Max Warren
LS 20/21	The Thirty-Nine Articles: Their Place and Use Today	Jim Packer, Roger Beckwith
LS 22	How We Got Our Prayer Book	T.W. Drury, Roger Beckwith
LS 23/24	Creation or Evolution: a False Antithesis?	Mike Poole, Gordon Wenham
LS 25	Christianity and the Craft	Gerard Moate
LS 26	ARCIC II and Justification	Alister McGrath
LS 27	The Challenge of the Housechurches	Tony Higton, Gilbert Kirby
LS 28	Communion for Children? The Current Debate	A. A. Langdon
LS 29/30	Theological Politics	Nigel Biggar
LS 31	Eucharistic Consecration in the First Four Centuries and its Implications for Liturgical Reform	Nigel Scotland
LS 32	A Christian Theological Language	Gerald Bray
LS 33	Mission in Unity: The Bible and Missionary Structures	Duncan McMann
LS 34	Stewards of Creation: Environmentalism in the Light of Biblical Teaching	Lawrence Osborn
LS 35/36	Mission and Evangelism in Recent Thinking: 1974–1986	Robert Bashford
LS 37	Future Patterns of Episcopacy: Reflections in Retirement	Stuart Blanch
LS 38	Christian Character: Jeremy Taylor and Christian Ethics Today	David Scott
LS 39	Islam: Towards a Christian Assessment	Hugh Goddard
LS 40	Liberal Catholicism: Charles Gore and the Question of Authority	G. F. Grimes
LS 41/42	The Christian Message in a Multi-faith Society	Colin Chapman
LS 43	The Way of Holiness 1: Principles	D. A. Ousley
LS 44/45	The Lambeth Articles	V. C. Miller
LS 46	The Way of Holiness 2: Issues	D. A. Ousley
LS 47	Building Multi-Racial Churches	John Root

Latimer Publications

LS 48	Episcopal Oversight: A Case for Reform	David Holloway
LS 49	Euthanasia: A Christian Evaluation	Henk Jochemsen
LS 50/51	The Rough Places Plain: AEA 1995	
LS 52	A Critique of Spirituality	John Pearce
LS 53/54	The Toronto Blessing	Martyn Percy
LS 55	The Theology of Rowan Williams	Garry Williams
LS 56/57	Reforming Forwards? The Process of Reception and the Consecration of Woman as Bishops	Peter Toon
LS 58	The Oath of Canonical Obedience	Gerald Bray
LS 59	The Parish System: The Same Yesterday, Today And For Ever?	Mark Burkill
LS 60	'I Absolve You': Private Confession and the Church of England	Andrew Atherstone
LS 61	The Water and the Wine: A Contribution to the Debate on Children and Holy Communion	Roger Beckwith, Andrew Daunton-Fear
LS 62	Must God Punish Sin?	Ben Cooper
LS 63	Too Big For Words? The Transcendence of God and Finite Human Speech	Mark D. Thompson
LS 64	A Step Too Far: An Evangelical Critique of Christian Mysticism	Marian Raikes
LS 65	The New Testament and Slavery: Approaches and Implications	Mark Meynell
LS 66	The Tragedy of 1662: The Ejection and Persecution of the Puritans	Lee Gatiss
LS 67	Heresy, Schism & Apostasy	Gerald Bray
LS 68	Paul in 3D: Preaching Paul as Pastor, Story-teller and Sage	Ben Cooper
LS69	Christianity and the Tolerance of Liberalism: J.Gresham Machen and the Presbyterian Controversy of 1922-1937	Lee Gatiss
LS70	An Anglican Evangelical Identity Crisis: The Churchman-Anvil Affair of 1981-4	Andrew Atherstone
LS71	Empty and Evil: The worship of other faiths in 1 Corinthians 8-10 and today	Rohintan Mody
LS72	To Plough or to Preach: Mission Strategies in New Zealand during the 1820s	Malcolm Falloon
LS73	Plastic People: How Queer Theory is changing us	Peter Sanlon
LS74	Deification and Union with Christ: Salvation in Orthodox and Reformed thought	Slavko Eždenci
LS75	As It Is Written: Interpreting the Bible with Boldness	Benjamin Sargent
LS76	Light From Dark Ages? An Evangelical Critique of Celtic Spirituality	Marian Raikes
LS77	The Ethics of Usury	Ben Cooper
LS78	For Us and For Our Salvation: 'Limited Atonement' in the Bible, Doctrine, History and Ministry	Lee Gatiss

Latimer Briefings

LB01	The Church of England: What it is, and what it stands for	R. T. Beckwith
LB02	Praying with Understanding: Explanations of Words and Passages in the Book of Common Prayer	R. T. Beckwith
LB03	The Failure of the Church of England? The Church, the Nation and the Anglican Communion	A. Pollard
LB04	Towards a Heritage Renewed	H.R.M. Craig
LB05	Christ's Gospel to the Nations: The Heart & Mind of Evangelicalism Past, Present & Future	Peter Jensen
LB06	Passion for the Gospel: Hugh Latimer (1485–1555) Then and Now. A commemorative lecture to mark the 450th anniversary of his martyrdom in Oxford	A. McGrath

Latimer Publications

LB07	Truth and Unity in Christian Fellowship	Michael Nazir-Ali
LB08	Unworthy Ministers: Donatism and Discipline Today	Mark Burkill
LB09	Witnessing to Western Muslims: A Worldview Approach to Sharing Faith	Richard Shumack
LB10	Scarf or Stole at Ordination? A Plea for the Evangelical Conscience	Andrew Atherstone
LB11	How to Write a Theology Essay	Michael P. Jensen
LB12	Preaching: A Beginner's Guidebook	Allan Chapple
LB13	Justification By Faith: Orientating the Church's teaching and practice to Christ	Michael Nazir-Ali
LB14	"Remember Your Leaders": Principles and Priorities for Leaders from Hebrews 13	Wallace Benn
LB15	How the Anglican Communion came to be and where it is going	Michael Nazir-Ali

Latimer Books

GGC	God, Gays and the Church: Human Sexuality and Experience in Christian Thinking	eds. Lisa Nolland, Chris Sugden, Sarah Finch
WTL	The Way, the Truth and the Life: Theological Resources for a Pilgrimage to a Global Anglican Future	eds. Vinay Samuel, Chris Sugden, Sarah Finch
AEID	Anglican Evangelical Identity – Yesterday and Today	J.I.Packer, N.T.Wright
IB	The Anglican Evangelical Doctrine of Infant Baptism	John Stott, Alec Motyer
BF	Being Faithful: The Shape of Historic Anglicanism Today	Theological Resource Group of GAFCON
TPG	The True Profession of the Gospel: Augustus Toplady and Reclaiming our Reformed Foundations	Lee Gatiss
SG	Shadow Gospel: Rowan Williams and the Anglican Communion Crisis	Charles Raven
TTB	Translating the Bible: From Willliam Tyndale to King James	Gerald Bray
PWS	Pilgrims, Warriors, and Servants: Puritan Wisdom for Today's Church	ed. Lee Gatiss
PPA	Preachers, Pastors, and Ambassadors: Puritan Wisdom for Today's Church	ed. Lee Gatiss
CWP	The Church, Women Bishops and Provision: The Integrity of Orthodox Objections to the Proposed Legislation Allowing Women Bishops	
TSF	The Truth Shall Set You Free: Global Anglicanism in the 21st Century	Ed. Charles Raven

Anglican Foundations Series

FWC	The Faith We Confess: An Exposition of the 39 Articles	Gerald Bray
AF02	The 'Very Pure Word of God': The Book of Common Prayer as a Model of Biblical Liturgy	Peter Adam
AF03	Dearly Beloved: Building God's People Through Morning and Evening Prayer	Mark Burkill
AF04	Day By Day: The Rhythm of the Bible in the Book of Common Prayer	Benjamin Sargent
AF05	The Supper: Cranmer and Communion	Nigel Scotland

If you have enjoyed this book, you might like to consider

- *supporting the work of the Latimer Trust*
- *reading more of our publications*
- *recommending them to others*

See www.latimertrust.org for more information.

www.ingramcontent.com/pod-product-compliance
Ingram Content Group UK Ltd.
Pitfield, Milton Keynes, MK11 3LW, UK
UKHW041306180426
11947UKWH00009B/710